PRAISE FOR POEMCITY

"This is poetry for the people, in the tradition of community and the spoken word…It's a beautiful book… There are poems for everyone in this anthology."

—*George Longenecker, in the Montpelier Bridge*

"I enjoyed *PoemCity Anthology 2023.* I read every poem— from Vermonters in towns and villages all across the state, young and old, various topics, life, death, daybreak, nightfall, working, dreaming, portraits of people, pets, cars, seed catalogs, olive oil, a glove, all the seasons, and feelings, joy, grief, love of course. I think there were more than 250 poems! Each one telling a story, uniquely Vermont, but universal, heartfelt."

—*Nancy Haiduck, Burlington*

"April is not the cruelest month in Montpelier because we have PoemCity. It is so uplifting to walk around town and see all the wonderful words that people have crafted."

—*Roberta Harold, Montpelier*

"How better to buoy your community and others than with poems from the heart."

—*Lily Hinrichsen, Bristol*

"I look forward once again to seeing the poetic diversity of Vermont, which is one thing that makes me happy to live here."

—*Sydney Lea, Vermont Poet Laureate 2011-15*

"I am excited to see how the poems reflect the year we had and to experience yet another example of art as a vehicle for communal healing."

—*Devon Parish, Montpelier*

"I'm so excited that I get to submit to PoemCity this year! I love that we have a unique way of showing our writers community, and I love sharing my poems."

—*Lydia Bearsch, Grade 6, Main Street Middle School*

"After all the ways that COVID and flooding have impacted our state, I'm looking forward to seeing Montpelier filled with poetry and people connecting with words and one another."

—*Deidra Razzaque, Brattleboro*

"PoemCity is part of Montpelier's heartbeat."

—*Candelin Wahl, Burlington*

POEMCITY ANTHOLOGY 2024

PoemCity ANTHOLOGY

• 2024 •

Kellogg-Hubbard
LIBRARY

Rootstock Publishing

Montpelier, Vermont

PoemCity Anthology 2024 is the second in an annual series
of PoemCity anthologies.

All Rights Reserved.

ISBN: 978-1-57869-167-8
eBook ISBN: 978-1-57869-172-2

Library of Congress Control Number: 2024933131

Published by Rootstock Publishing
an imprint of Ziggy Media LLC
Montpelier, VT 05602
info@rootstockpublishing.com
www.rootstockpublishing.com

Compiled by The Kellogg-Hubbard Library
135 Main Street, Montpelier, VT 05502
info@kellogghubbard.org
www.kellogghubbard.org

Designed by Dana Dwinell-Yardley (ddydesign.com).

Cover Art: "Slowly Wade," a digital illustration
by Fiona Perez Razzaque ©2023.

Printed in the USA.

Dedicated to
Reuben Jackson (1956–2024),
poet, educator, jazz scholar, radio DJ, music critic,
and Vermonter at heart.

CONTENTS

Introduction i

Acknowledgments ii

PART 1: POEMS

Forsythian 3
Rick Agran, Worcester

The Music 4
Bonnie Alexander, Montpelier

The Large and the Small 5
Glo Alexander, Montpelier

Hope is a Voice 6
Amy Allen, Shelburne

Avian Mantle 7
Garet Allen-Malley, Montpelier

The Way 8
Meg Boisseau Allison, Moretown

New Pasture 9
Kyla Allon, Montpelier

The Poacher 10
Ina Anderson, South Royalton

Tracks 11
Cara Meyer Lovell Arduengo, Barre

Seeing Vinnie Off 12
Barb Asen, Montpelier

Tree Frogs 13
S. Atwood, East Montpelier

Transformations of Matter 14
D. Slayton Avery, Woodbury

Spring Memory 15
Doreen Spencer Ballard,
South Woodstock

fall 16
Meadow Baptiste, Cabot

Fiddleheads 17
Charles Barasch, Plainfield

Keep Pace 18
Julia Barstow, East Montpelier

The Chicken 19
Linden Basor, age 11, Calais

Chickens 20
Talia Kilian, age 10, Barre Town,
and Linden Basor, age 11, Calais

Girlfriend Secrets 21
Susan K. Bauchner, Warren

Dawn 22
Colleen Beamish, Barre

Becoming 23
Lydia Bearsch, age 11, Montpelier

November 24
Jean Beatson, Jericho

Neighborhood Forum
Ghazal 25
Sarah Birgé, Montpelier

Spinning Sun from Winter
Days 26
Chelsea Blackwell, East Montpelier

Who Paints the Flowers 28
Adam Boothe, Burlington

One Girl and Two Roses 29
Amelie Boucher, age 8,
East Montpelier

Sustenance 30
Catherine Boudreau, Worcester

Internal Storm 31
Alethea Bouton, Quechee

Untitled 32
Becky Bowen, Montpelier

Admiring Downy Woodpecker's
Black and White Feathers 33
Anne Bower, South Pomfret

Made Make More 34
Scott Boyd, Stowe

Kitchen Karaoke   35
Donna Bramley, South Burlington

Who-cooks-for-you?   36
Mark Brown, East Calais

Me and My Brother   37
Thomas Brown, age 11, East Calais

Indigeneity   38
Megan Buchanan, Putney

We Are This   39
Ed Burke, Brattleboro

We All Fall Down   40
wayne f. burke, Barre

Driving Lessons V   41
Ana Burtnett, Worcester

Karen Carpenter   42
Jolynda Burton, Montpelier

Wednesday, 2:00, Physical
Therapy: *Between Exercises,
Bobble Your Head*   43
Sue D. Burton, Burlington

Sister Stars   44
Patricia Louise Joi Canada, Barre

Everyone has Written a Poem
About a Winter's Night   46
Kathleen Casserly, Montpelier

"Be Your Own Boss"   47
Dave Cavanagh, Burlington

On Finding Old Age
Unfathomable   48
Judith Chalmer, Burlington

By the light of winter   49
Samuel L. Chambers, Essex Junction

December 5th   50
Shianne Charette, Cabot

It's Poetry Month   51
Mary Cheyne, Chelsea

The Comfort of a Gray Day   52
Susan Chickering, East Montpelier

February 9, 2023   53
Alice Christian, Colchester

Stuck in a Good Book   54
Lexi Clarfeld, age 8, Colchester

Dream in the Wilderness:
John Clarke Barker, 1851   55
Peter L. Clark, Woodbury

Singer at the Well of Souls   56
Peter Clark, Woodbury

Daytime   57
*Conor Isaiah Cleveland,
Williamstown*

The Champlain Sea   58
PH Coleman, South Burlington

velvet curtains   59
Mary L. Collins, Lake Elmore

The Act of Love   60
Ann Cooper, Middlebury

Nigh the Waters   61
Linda Corelia, Montpelier

hearing the phoebe:
Five Haiku for the Year   62
Nichael Cramer, Guilford

Ledger   63
Stephen Cramer, Burlington

Sunflower   64
James Crews, Shaftsbury

Slip Away   65
Jezebel Crow, Woodbury

Winter Apple Trees   66
Terri Crowther, Washington

The Juniata's waters   67
Ralph Culver, South Burlington

I heard you were back   68
Douglas K. Currier, Winooski

Diminished   69
daithí, Montpelier

What if Grocery Store   70
W. Dall, Montpelier

Ancient Oak   72
Corinne Davis, Montpelier

Kindred Solitude 73
Sarah E. DeBouter, Berlin

A Promise for Spring 74
Grace Decker, Burlington

To Our Indolent Cancer 75
Greg Delanty, Burlington

The Anthropocene,
Montpelier Vermont 76
nd dentico, East Montpelier

Pruning the Apple Trees 77
Deborah Dickerson, Bristol

Apricity 78
Monica DiGiovanni, Montpelier

July 4th, 2023 79
Arlene Iris Distler, Brattleboro

What Remains 80
Mariessa Dobrick, Barre

Inheritance 81
Jared Duval, Montpelier

It Is the Light 82
Maggie Eaton, East Montpelier

Jelly Donut 83
Kathryn Eberly, Montpelier

A Trick of the Light
Miraculous 84
Krikmöklet Egelanaard, Chelsea

The Catch 85
Nietzsche Danann Egelanaard,
Chelsea

Be By Myself 86
Ezra, age 3, Colchester

December storm 87
buzz ferver, Berlin

A Drink of Field 88
Ann Fisher, Lincoln

The Connecticut 89
Michael Fleming, Brattleboro

Batten Kill Through
Mill Pond 90
Julia H. Fonte, Poultney

Bones 91
Elias Kai Francis, Williamstown

Bittersweet Still Life 92
Sarah Franklin, Montpelier

In Trust 93
debby franzoni, Castleton

so much more in common 94
david fried, Montpelier

Wake of the Flood 95
Gaia Fried, Montpelier

Stilt Walking 97
Navah Fried, South Burlington

Judgments 98
Marcy Frink, Worcester

Pledge 99
Jamie Gage, Stockbridge

Blessed Life 100
Harriet Galfetti, Berlin

Chronic 101
Claire Gallagher, Barre

The Afternoon Porch in the
Morning 102
Walt Garner, West Brookfield

Untitled 103
Susan Gerretson, Montpelier

passing by 104
Brian Goodwin, Middlesex

A flash flood always begins with
a drop of rain on a stone* 105
Andrea Gould, Plainfield

The Maple 106
Sara Graham, Barre

Envious Moon 107
William Graham, Stowe

Making Paella in America 108
Gail Grycel, Westminster West

Muscle memory 109
Jennifer Gundy, Marshfield

First Mud Season in
Vermont   110
N.G. Haiduck, Burlington

The Last Man to Die for a
Mistake   111
Roberta Harold, Montpelier

Undoing   112
Tracy Haught, Montpelier

Visitors from the Permafrost 113
Jen Heller, Montpelier

Shelter   114
Kathleen Herrington, Montpelier

Skunk Diplomacy   115
Sam Hewitt, Essex Junction

Wandering sorrow   116
Cindy Ellen Hill, Middlebury

Winter's Song   117
Alicia Hingston, Danville

If   118
Lily Hinrichsen, Bristol

Back to the Sea   119
Linda Hogan, Montpelier

Sew and Tell   120
Linda Hogan, Montpelier

Halfway in Between   121
Jim Hogue, Graniteville

When It Rains in January,
Go to the Movies   123
Michelle Fay Holder, Montpelier

Ghost Dance   124
Sarah Hooker, Marshfield

Long Distance Love   125
Reuben Jackson (1956–2024),
Vermonter at Heart

Comprehend   126
Jacob, Cabot

Beekeeping   127
Mary Elder Jacobsen, North Calais

Searching for the Light   128
Joan Javier-Duval, Montpelier

Crown Our Tomorrows   129
Anna N. Jennings, West Towshend

Freya   130
Malachi Johns, age 9, Roxbury

Sledding   131
Jade Johns, age 11, Roxbury

Awake   132
Juniper Johns, Roxbury

First Collision   133
Daniel Johnson, Burlington

I Want to Know Someone
Who Calls Me Kitten   134
(Robyn) Joy, Montpelier

Immaculate Reception   135
Phil Keller, Montpelier

At Townshend Beach   136
Monda R. Kelley, Brandon

24 Questions about Love   138
David Klein, Montpelier

Threading the Needle   139
Tricia Knoll, Williston

Trimeter After Flood   140
Samantha Kolber, Montpelier

"Let the way be your seat
of honor"   141
Kristine Korman, Warren

Walk   142
Ava Lafferty, Lyndonville

We Must Tend Our
Beautiful Earth   143
Mayla Landis-Marinello, Middlesex

Invitation   144
M. Latoundji, Walden

Shadows   145
Sydney Lea, Newbury

The Old   146
Maxine Leary, Montpelier

Boreal (Entropy)   147
Maggie Lenz, Montpelier

1-10 (and Back Again)   148
Michael Levine, Middlesex

PoemCity   149
craig line, Calais

Casting Seeds   150
Lisa, East Montpelier

Love Poem to a Library   151
George Longenecker, Middlesex

About Grief   152
Jesse LoVasco, East Montpelier

Nothing You Need   153
Daniel Lusk, Burlington

Family   154
River M., Cabot

Reflected Light   155
Sandra Maccarrone, Montpelier

Almanac   156
Michael Madill, West Topsham

Mortal Down   157
Kimberly Madura, Essex

Leaving Iowa City /
The Right Questions   158
Jack Markoski, Montpelier

Take Blue   159
Katherine H. Maynard, South
Burlington

The Legacy of Elms   160
Tim Mayo, Brattleboro

Tree of Solitude   161
Elizabeth McCarthy, Walden

In your next letter   162
Florence McCloud, South Burlington

Mother-In-Law in the Bardo   163
Hatsy McGraw, Hartland

Winter, Vermont   164
Kelly McMahon, Montpelier

In the Nest of Night   165
Rebecca McMeekin, Braintree

At My Sister's   166
Joanne Mellin, Winooski

Silver Maple Story   167
Christine Corrigan Mendez,
Burlington

Luna Moth   168
Christy Mihaly, East Calais

Shoe Laces   169
Steve Minkin, Brattleboro

Broken   170
Benjamin L. Mitchell, Westminster

Reverberation   171
Richard W. Moore, Burlington

For Poetry   172
Karen Morris, Barre

The Stag   173
Nicola Morris, Plainfield

November   174
B. Morrison, Brattleboro

Deer on the move: Road Sign
on I 91, November   175
Barbara E. Murphy, Burlington

life for life   176
elizabeth murmuring, Barre

A Snow Squall Arrives   177
Joan Murray, Worcester

long distance   178
Beck Natale, Colchester

The Summer of Smoke   179
Erika Nichols-Frazer, Waitsfield

Even the dreams of
James Joyce   180
Nitya, Barre

A Perfect Day   181
Penny Nolte, Montpelier

ocean grove   182
Travis Alden Nutting, Middlesex

Ten-Day Silent Retreat   183
Kevin O'Keefe, West Brattleboro

Bilingual (Japanese/English)
Tankas 184
Michiko Oishi, Montpelier

Grandpa 185
Richard Fischer Olson, Montpelier

Something to that Effect 186
Ann Onymous, Moscow

To my slow toddler 187
Holly Painter, South Burlington

Jane Doe 188
Emma Paris, Putney

Free Pile 189
Devon Parish, Montpelier

Beluga 190
Scudder H. Parker, Middlesex

Homesteading in Vermont 191
Rolf Parker-Houghton, Brattleboro

On The La Platte 192
Angela Patten, Burlington

January 193
Melissa Perley, Berlin

Spelling the News 194
Verandah Porche, Guilford

Heartbeat 195
Sean Prentiss, Woodbury

Long Love 196
Alison Prine, Burlington

Love at first sight 197
Parvathi Rajaram, Montpelier

Worksong 198
Kiev Rattee, Manchester

Afternoon at Sea 199
Deidra K. Razzaque, Brattleboro

At The Last 200
Susan Reid, Montpelier

The spray of lilies 201
Susan Reid, Montpelier

Love Is 202
Vera Resnik, Warren

Aquamarine 203
Michael Roach, Montpelier

December Blues 204
Greg Robertson, Northfield

Nature 205
Margo Robertson, age 9, Northfield

Then Dust 206
Bruce Jefferson Rose, Monkton

Evening from a Window 207
Andrew Ross, Montpelier

A good death 208
Jenny Rossi, Winooski

Reflecting on Robert Bly's
Silence in the Snowy Fields 209
Charles Rossiter, Bennington

Returning Home 210
Aysha Mae Russell, Marshfield

Beach Dancing 211
*Martha Anderson Sanborn,
Vergennes*

Aging 212
Sam Sanders, Montpelier

Invisible Matters 213
Susan M. Sanders, Burlington

Before My Homeland Had
a Name 214
Kelly Sargent, Williston

Women's Circles 215
Nancy Scarcello, Florence

That Old Story 216
Gail Marlene Schwartz, Montpelier

The Door 217
Rachel Senechal, East Montpelier

July Fever 218
Aurora Sharp, Moretown

29 October 2023   219
L V M Shelton, Montpelier

Ways We Like Onion River
Outdoors!   220
Helen Shoesmith, age 9, Montpelier

Something to rise   221
Rebecca Siegel, Thetford Center

Watch/Warning/Flood   222
Michelle A.L. Singer, East Montpelier

Reflections While Fishing   223
Grant Smith, Montpelier

Beech   224
*Martha E. Snell, El Cerrito,
California*

Nothing in Nature
is Simple   225
*Martha E. Snell, El Cerrito,
California*

The Wonder   226
*Martha E. Snell, El Cerrito,
California*

When You Visit   227
sb sōwbel, Montpelier

Working Mother   228
Katie Spring, Worcester

Blues for the Masses   229
Toussaint St. Negritude, Newark

Together   230
*Heather Stearns,
White River Junction*

Prescient   231
Samn Stockwell, Barre

Water, Life's Partner!   232
Yvonne Straus, Montpelier

Ode to a Lioness   233
*Ashley Anne Strobridge |
Astrobridge Artistry, Montpelier*

Orchard   235
Lynn Parrish Sutton, Burlington

Beginning with One Stone   236
Pamela Tallmadge, Colchester

Haiku: snow and ice   237
Geza Tatrallyay, Barnard

Dreaming Sky   238
Ella Thomas, Calais

Secret   239
Leilah Thompson, Cabot

Now   240
T T Tomlinson, Essex Junction

Twice   241
Robert Troester, Montpelier

Noise canceling   242
Tamsen Turner, East Calais

Reaching Ken   243
Betsy Unger, Montpelier

The Guest Book   244
Candelin Wahl, Burlington

Reverse Heroics   245
Janet Watton, Randolph Center

Two Roberts   246
*JC Wayne | Creative for Good,
Charlotte*

Black Birds   247
Sharon Webster, Burlington

Cathedral   248
Diana Whitney, Brattleboro

Creation   249
Emily A. Wills, Fairfax

Tree of Life   250
M. Wilson, Barre

When the Second Person
Dies*   251
Heather Wishik, Woodstock

Cirrostratus   252
Shyloh Wonder-Maez, Barre

Transient Breath   253
James W. Wyman, Alburgh

Among Canards   254
Martha Zweig, Hardwick

PART 2: SCHOOLS

CALAIS
ELEMENTARY SCHOOL

Samantha Jackson's Third
and Fourth Grade Class   256

MAIN STREET MIDDLE
SCHOOL, MONTPELIER

Kiki Adams's
Fifth Grade Class   269

Debbie Goodwin's
Fifth Grade Class   274

Windy Kelley's
Fifth Grade Class   289

Wendy McGuiggan's
Fifth Grade Class   297

Melissa Parker's
Fifth Grade Class   308

Animal Poems   316

Introduction

PoemCity, the Kellogg-Hubbard Library's annual celebration of National Poetry Month in April, celebrates its fifteenth year in 2024. For a decade and a half, Montpelier has been the smallest capital city in the U.S. with the biggest celebration of National Poetry Month. We have an amazing community of poets from all corners of the state and from a wide range of experience: for some, this is their first poem; for others, their hundredth.

To love Vermont is nothing new. However, there is a special quality to being able to walk through an anthology of poetry, stopping to read the poems of our neighbors and friends while we pick up a coffee, shop, bank, and countless other tasks. It is made possible by the poets, the downtown businesses, the Kellogg-Hubbard Library staff and volunteers, and our sponsors: Vermont Humanities, Hunger Mountain Coop, and Rootstock Publishing. For the second time ever, we have collected PoemCity's poems into a printed volume that can be enjoyed all year and anywhere. We hope you enjoy this celebration of community and poetry as much as we do.

—*Michelle Singer, Coordinator of PoemCity 2024*

ACKNOWLEDGMENTS

The Kellogg-Hubbard Library would like to thank the following individuals for their help with this anthology: Dana Dwinell-Yardley, Marisa Keller, Samantha Kolber, and Michelle Singer.

Special thanks to Rachel Senechal and Phayvanh Luekhamhan for creating PoemCity, formally PoetryALIVE!, fifteen years ago. Many volunteers over the years have made PoemCity possible, as well as our community partners and downtown Montpelier business owners—our heartfelt thanks go to them. Generous support from Vermont Humanities, and the Hunger Mountain Coop has made PoemCity thrive.

Another special thanks to Fiona Perez Razzaque for the cover art, which Fiona created as an artistic response to Deidra Razzaque's poem "Afternoon at Sea" on page 199.

Finally, thank you to all the poets and readers.
The following poems have been printed as submitted with permission.

Poems

Forsythian

The little neighbor girl parks her red and white tricycle
on the hill next to my blooming forsythia

& crawls under the bushes' golden dome
formed by drooping winter-burnished branches.

She lies on her back. Goldfinches hop back & forth overhead,
& sing to her: *zweep-zweep, po-ta-to chips, po-ta-to chips...*

a blue skyful of minuscule yellow trumpets play along above
& she feels it in the hollows of her collarbones, under

her small ribs, her heart pounding & under this golden dome
of weeping, her tears spend themselves, filling her ears

as goldfinches settle in quiet witness...   She shakes her head
to empty her ears & finds an equilibrium in even breathing

then decamps in a burst of yellow petals & startled darting
    finches,
remounts her trike & rolls off down the hill.

—*Rick Agran, Worcester*

The Music

Music, a thing of grace and style
Engulfing the mind
Surround the heart music and I
Never part never part
Never part
Apart from this, our world
Should be an utter travesty.

—*Bonnie Alexander, Montpelier*

The Large and the Small

The larger one gets, the slower time passes.
The smaller one gets, time it speeds up.
If everything is then equally shrunk or expanded,
no one would notice that anything's changed,
but if even one thread then refuses compliance,
the time line is altered and an unbalance corrupts.
Scale is the measure that proves this is true, $E=MC$ squared
    and how much is used,
for life in a doll house passes much faster than life in a castle
    of giants who wear
ginormous size shoes, they take a few steps and go a great
    distance,
then wee folk e'er could travel in no shorter time.
Measuring hours and minutes and seconds,
The shape of time telling is not the same in each land.
Yet the sun in the sky doesn't care how little or big,
only shadows cast change the way we perceive.

—Glo Alexander, Montpelier

Hope is a Voice

for Amanda Gorman

When hatred spilled over into unbridled rage
when fists and clubs were lifted skyward,
there was despair in who we had become
in who we actually were
in how foolish we had been
to think otherwise.

And yet, up to the podium
stepped a brilliant and vibrant light
giving us permission to lift our heads
giving voice to all that we had been carrying
giving us something to once again believe in
giving air to finally breathe again

and so we stepped tentatively together
once more back toward the light
our spirits buoyed by the irrefutable truth
that words matter
that poetry matters
that hope is a dazzling young woman
guiding us united
up the hill we must climb.

—Amy Allen, Shelburne

Avian Mantle

                                        Surging
                                out
                        of the
                eastern
        sky
        a

phalanx of crows
hundreds strong

        land
        en masse

in the ancient pin oak

        cloaking
        bare limbs
in shimmering ebony.

—*Garet Allen-Malley, Montpelier*

The Way

My offering only this—
> an ancient echo vibrating inside the Milky Way;
> > *this too shall pass.*

Mother earth will continue to spin on her axis around the sun,
> casting shadows both undulating and blunt;
the face of the moon will continue to wax and wane overhead,
> in absence of praise;
the stars will continue to silently blink,
> their refractions birthing new creation stories.

Seeds will push up from underneath,
> like newborn heads crowning.
The hatchling will open its beak,
> in need of its mother's bile.
The infant,—or calf,—or fawn, will suckle from the teat,
> within seconds upon arrival.

We shall navigate toward our sustenance—
> a certain slant of light,
> > a mouthful of worms,
> > > a ribbon of milk.

—*Meg Boisseau Allison, Moretown*

New Pasture

With rain in our eyes, voices high, and arms outstretched,
like parishioners calling to God,
we moved the sheep forward
to the new pasture.

All but one lamb made it;

sick and tired, she lay in the high grass,
hooves folded beneath her, eyes closed.

I went to her, cradling her head
and wondering out loud
where she would like to be brought
for her last breath.

We left her by a twisted apple tree
that shielded her from the rain,
allowing her to sleep
as she drifted between worlds.

—*Kyla Allon, Montpelier*

The Poacher

After dark there'd be a soft
knock at the door.
"I'll get it." said my Mum.
Taking her handbag with her,
she went to lift the latch.

"A coupla nice ones tonight, Mrs Baker."
He grinned and reached down inside
his tall black wellies, drew out
two large dark salmon, eyes bulging,
still hopelessly gulping at the air.

"Ooh, those *are* nice!" whispered Mum,
reaching inside her purse, "Ten shillings?"
and "Yes," he said, "that'll do nicely,"
as his smile faded out the door,
back into the night.

—*Ina Anderson, South Royalton*
from *Journey Into Space*, Antrim House

Tracks

When I look down
at my trodding boots—
a sign
  of another foot
    delicate claw points
        space   of a leap—
          then a landing. Paws
            sinking smoothly
           into snow,
             then joining the trail
               mixed, matted, mushed
  when I look down
at my trodding boots.

—*Cara Meyer Lovell Arduengo, Barre*

Seeing Vinnie Off

There in the mist, a rumble, a blur
an emerging figure
in changing light and conditions
that shroud unshroud reshroud it.

A shift in taste and prickle on skin,
and again it recedes
waiting,
gathering until it
lurches out of the fog
and shows the beauty You must embrace
a finite number of times.

We say the relationship continues
and parting at death
is also illusion;

so the heart is pared open, stung
squishy with gratitude,
longing, belonging,
releasing,   left

a knotted tapestry of remembering.

—*Barb Asen, Montpelier*

Tree Frogs

Tree frogs, I think three this evening,
are cronking in the nearby wood,
taking me back to the time of small feet,
high grass and fireflies,
just as the cricket call in August signals change,
a small wave of grief washes over
the day when the grass in the fields stops growing
and songbirds grow quiet,
and the child went to bed in the twilight
soon to be darkness, but now the tree frogs,
their ancient song, the ancient child,
this summer evening,
the way we are enfolded
not just moving forward and alone.

—S. Atwood, *East Montpelier*

Transformations of Matter

don't think me shiftless

I'm bearing witness

to the melting snow

transformations of matter

microscopic multifold

crystalline structures collapse

heaped snow shrinks and shifts

drips water and mist

changing shape and form

winter's end is this

snow a splitting chrysalis

spring unfolds damp wings

—D. Slayton Avery, Woodbury

previously published online at shiftnshake.wordpress.com

Spring Memory

My hands dig into
a mixture of dry bagged compost,
create a pile on the makeshift table,
plywood on sawhorses.
After all these years of gardening,
nothing permanent, but it works well
for breaking apart round, hard clumps,
dry blocks of organic matter.

The smell brings me back.
I am once again standing
in the center of the potting shed.
My mother in her work dress,
a flowered kerchief holding her dark hair,
packs soil in shallow flats,
pokes holes in the rich mixture
with her wooden dowel,
makes new homes for tender growing plants.

—Doreen Spencer Ballard, South Woodstock

fall

found poem: source text: "The 'Apple' of the Media's Eye: Burtt's Orchard in the News," the Cabot Chronicle, October 2022

fall,
orchards
tasty apple cider
delicious fruits
tree grow happy
maple trees
wild apples
playing games
fall tending the right way
right flavor of apple cider donuts
pumpkins
my favorite time of year is fall
families and kids enjoying the harvest
I like to breathe in the fall season
hard to say goodbye to this year

—Meadow Baptiste, Cabot

Fiddleheads

Along the roadside
hundreds of fiddleheads,
half-unfurled, huddle
in conclaves of five or six,
solemn heads bowed,
conversing like tiny priests.
Listen—they babble of philosophy
and the arts, of resurrection,
of sniffing muddy streams
and apple blossoms,
talking fast because soon
they will unclench
and become magnificent
silent peacocks.

—Charles Barasch, Plainfield

Keep Pace

Dry ground bristles under
your summer tough feet,
tomatoes swell taut in green skins,
yarrow dries on the stalk. Winter
shouts at your doorstep,
at your too small wood pile,
at your screens still in the window frames,
at the garlic unplanted,
the apples left for windfalls.

How you started to run
with the pace of spring snow melt,
to flush with the red ripe berries,
to waterfall through the abundance,
and slow only after all else has.

You are full and not yet fearful
of what is already here
and long to stay.

—*Julia Barstow, East Montpelier*

The Chicken

The chicken clucks to say hello,
As you hear the rooster crow.
Chickens squawk and flap and run,
Under the bright white blazing sun.
The chicken lays some eggs and sits,
Twenty days later there are some chicks.
I feed the little chicks right from my hand,
Soon they will grow and be out on the land.
I hold the chicken and feel its heat,
In my hands I feel its heart beat.
Cluck, crow, peep—all day long;
These noises are the chickens' song.

—*Linden Basor, age 11, Calais*

Chickens

Cluck-cluck, bak-bak!
Hens lay eggs.
In the egg lies a chick.
Chicks go peep-peep.
King of the coop, the rooster crows.
Early in the morning, the chickens are awake.
New chicks come every spring.
Soon the chicks will grow.

—Talia Kilian, age 10, Barre Town, and Linden Basor, age 11, Calais

Girlfriend Secrets

Hearts opened
That day
Around this table

Our stories,
Never before shared,
Spilled from our lips

We listened in awe
Hearing stories
That felt like our own

A deep commonality emerged
Compassion and connection
Bound us in caring

Freed from our secrets
Understood, perhaps loved,
We held each other

For our honesty
And our courage
I am grateful

—*Susan K. Bauchner, Warren*

Dawn

I wanted to watch the sun rise,
but I couldn't see the sun, so instead
I watched the sky awaken.

She said good morning,
I stretched,
and said hello.

The bustling birds sang along and the complaining cow rioted.

Dear world, please stay asleep,
just for today.
Let the birds have this day for their own.

—*Colleen Beamish, Barre*

Becoming

As a gust of winter breeze blows and for a second,
I become something, someone
I hope I grow to love.
Because inside I see my future,
The great, warm winter nights,
The sweet summer ice cream,
And me,
Looking back,
Cherishing this wonderful,
Powerful moment inside my mind,
And I believe that becoming myself,
Will be an adventure inside and out.
And the traits I pick up along the way,
Will make me,

Me.

—*Lydia Bearsch, age 11, Montpelier*

November

A lone woman sits
in the graveyard
of her dreams.
A barren tree
her companion and soulmate.
Ghosts of her unborn children
murmur forever elusive.

She loves November's
cold hard greys.
No fraudulently beautiful snow,
no green flaunting impossible promise,
no hypnotically brilliant colors.

She leans against the tree and sighs,
as the earth enfolds her
and the howling wind
sings her song.

—*Jean Beatson, Jericho*

Neighborhood Forum Ghazal

Are YOU missing a clear frozen jug?
I found milk (whole, yours?) on Cherry Avenue.

A pedestrian crow, tapping at its pebbled plastic,
found it cooler on the claws than asphalt Cherry Avenue.

My dog stole your milk from the crow
(highwaymen are rife up on Cherry Avenue).

He mouthed the handle and brought it to me melting dairy
reeking round Cherry Avenue.

Enraged by crime and beauty, I kicked your whole milk
    down Cherry Avenue;
it burst and bloomed all pearly over Cherry Avenue.

—*Sarah Birgé, Montpelier*

Spinning Sun from Winter Days

Sun lies hidden. How to spin light from what we have on hand?

Gather to our lips citrus, calabaza, Solanaceae.
Seeds and cells and stars so delicately holding sunshine past.

Bring the body near flowing water, her song will cheer you.

Search the sky doggedly, not without humor, for any
    possible signs of light.
Let those golden crumbs melt on your tongue.

Rest.
No arguments. Just do it. Even minute doses heal.

Rest also yields dreamwork.
Sunshine over bright beaches in your brain, dappled on
    inner forest paths,
the wing of a Morphean bird set a-shimmer.

Be with People.
Both complain and refrain from complaining about the
    absence of Sun.
It helps and it does not help, and something about that is
    right and good.

Revel.
You know what to do. Sing, dance, laugh, strum the strings
    and strike the skins.
Care not, how it looks or sounds.
Be wild and free. The Sun loves wild and free.

If anything will tip the celestial scales it will be revelry.
Tickling Sun's sweet belly in such a way that politeness is
    forgotten
and the thick silver blankets of cloud are booty-shaken away.

When the light does pour out,
infinite will be the blue, wild and free will the snow crystals
    sparkle,
and boundless will be our joy.

—*Chelsea Blackwell, East Montpelier*

Who Paints the Flowers

Who paints the flowers
On electric boxes
That power the lives
We don't control or ask for?

Who pulls the horns
In highway trucks
For the unwatched kids
Using windows for wonder?

Who scrawls the words
On uneven sidewalks
That counterbalance
The easy lies we carry?

Who hides the art
Found alone on walks
That inspires us
To make a new secret place?

—*Adam Boothe, Burlington*

One Girl and Two Roses

1.

The world can be
scary but we will
survive and love
keeps us alive.
Life is different
every second.

Imagine a rose.

2.

Roses bloom and light will
shine night will come and
night will go.

3.

Darkness approaches me and
the world closes in on me but I run
as fast as I can and I walk the bridge.

—Amelie Boucher, age 8, East Montpelier

Sustenance

Above me—the sound of beating wings.

I cup a hand to my brow, look up
as a giant raven, for a moment,
blocks the sun, cawing.
It flies erratically, trying to dodge
the mob of smaller birds that attack,
all the while screaming out.

I turn back to the garden, where I am planting beets,
seeds like tiny grenades, all bumpy and brown.
It's hard to believe something so sweet looks the way a beet
    does.
I think it would be one of the more elegant vegetables—
like the delicate curling pea, or the feathery fennel.
But it is a dirty root, covered in a thick skin that needs
    peeling.

Cabbage moths—those tiny white wisps—
dance around the kale—
the leaves riddled with holes.
They look so pretty in their destruction.

What deceit Mother Nature is up to!

—*Catherine Boudreau, Worcester*

Internal Storm

There is no pressure on my chest,
No tears behind my eyes,
No anxious thoughts that wrest
Strident, unheard cries
Muffled in a clasp of dread.
No sinful, slowly rotting lies;
No tangled, twisted threads
Pretending to be quick and wise,
Tainted colors clenched in pain,
Sit in the dark within my head.
No hot stroke of frustration
Curves quickly down my spine;
No bruise-colored agitation,
No smile and pain combined.
No knot of empty hunger,
No hurt and angry mind.
No cement-like, frozen blood,
No heavy limbs and heart.
No, I am numb and faultless, cold,
A storm tearing me apart.

—*Alethea Bouton, Quechee*

The Rose of my dreams,
Guiding you, preparing you,
Mother's love takes flight.

—*Becky Bowen, Montpelier*

Admiring Downy Woodpecker's
Black and White Feathers

Rummage around and find elegant plumage,
something to salvage, drape over my rage,
hide seam-bursting baggage, the scars of life's damage,
messes and missteps, the unsorted garbage.

You'd think at this stage,
nearing last decades' passage
I'd accept tattered feathers, these signs of old age,
embrace wise crone's message
that cycles of nature are wondrous not carnage,
find easy way to turn a new page.

Rummage, remember riches at hand,
grasp what's here for a comforting garment,
warm, with folds that drape and flow.
Here's blue-sky's abundant silk,
winter-linen of bleached sunflower stalks,
sturdy cotton grays of old stone walls,
rough tan wool from stubbled fields,
knit with tai chi's slow steps and turns
into my silver, shining cloak.

—*Anne Bower, South Pomfret*

Made Make More

2 things specific more make
cliche made good
made make things
cliche more specific
good more make
specific specific.

Allegro and Andante
they know what they want
lemon tarts, snowflakes
in Vienna and pale, little
shells hoarded on every
beach by every sea.

Interlude

Driving there now
with the new Land Rover
curling tracks on the sands
sunglasses and a ponytail
iced rosé and clams
clams on the half shell.

A cliche made then
more but good like
pink wine and a raw
clam on the beach and
sunglasses in the sand
with the ponytail thing.

Interlude

Made more more
you specific cliche you
with your new Land Rover
making it good with
2 things and all those
tarts in Vienna.

More more made make
snowflake specific 2
but but make it good
curl tracks on the beach
make it Andante
made make more specific.

—*Scott Boyd, Stowe*

Kitchen Karaoke

Counter tops are not just for cooking anymore! My
Karaoke machine fits just fine and allows the convenience
of height and access for when I need my daily sing fix!
Although I'm somewhat of a Foodie I prefer singing in my
kitchen rather than cooking.

Having become proficient at Belting out a Cornucopia of
Rock tunes, I embrace the sound and enthusiasm I hear!
This is so much fun! I'm exploding with excitement and
savoring every moment I get to do this.

Is it the Kitchen? Why do I feel, taste, smell the pungent
aroma of those lyrics? I'm in the moment, groovin, singing,
dancing, baking in the heat of the song! Oh, if they could
see me now! My heart is full, like sprinkles of confection on
a gumdrop tree!

My day is complete, my attitude sweet, I'm happy now!
    Bon Appetit'.

Kitchen Karaoke!

—*Donna Bramley, South Burlington*

Who-cooks-for-you?

Shadow and claw and spine.
In a pine-spiked night,
       skittering.
If light, then cut to shafts passing.
       Unseated,
       breath at angles,
       noise tumbling toward distraction.
       Driven, shaken, shorn.
Snow seeps between blades—
       a melt,
       a freeze,
       foundering unsheltered in the dark
Beneath wings descending silence

—*Mark Brown, East Calais*

Me and My Brother

Hopping and skipping and
jumping and running,
Crashing and bashing and
smashing and clashing

Round and round the
little feet go,
Here and there,
to and fro.

This continuous ruckus
is around in the day.
But at night it's so quiet,
there's nothing to say.

Everything's silent
while sleeping.
Bodies at rest,
minds peacefully dreaming

But when you wake up
why, what happens then?
Everything starts
all over again.

—*Thomas Brown, age 11, East Calais*

Indigeneity

One of our own, he said

This pond, the stones, the forest,
the nettles, the stream, the birds,
the wind, the soil, the moss,
the gorse, the linnet, the sheep,
the sky, the land itself
says something like yes
something like home
it's cellular
emotional
clear

         a oneness

Beyond happiness, something else

—*Megan Buchanan, Putney*

We Are This

We are lovers
we are lovers
we love
each other
  forever
    is
  is each
touch, smile
gentle kindness,
affirmation
  is each
word, meant
caring, listening
listened, heard
each touch
faceted, of a whole

the calm
  the sea
within my ribs
the tides
the rise and ebb
the time now,
  to come
unknown, the light
  the radiance
inspired, held
offered, reflected
  received
cherished, cherished
    we
  are this
we are this

—*Ed Burke, Brattleboro*

We All Fall Down

A revolt of the leaves today.
Whirlwinds of yellow and rust-colored
rushing from one side of the street
to the other
like a mob
storming a Bastille.
But then lying down,
spent
apparently
until they get up
and renew the rush
only in a different direction,
obviously confused,
in chaos;
a tornado of them in the road
run through by a truck,
scattered;
they are a spiritual force
mainly
though make a clatter on sidewalks
like tiny horses' hooves scuttling—
like the clouds
not sure where they are going
either.

—*wayne f. burke, Barre*
previously published in *The Aurorean*, 2018

Driving Lessons V

"Pull over, son, make sure he can see your hands"
Your boy suddenly 15 maneuvers onto the uneven shoulder
You've been his helmsman for so long
Did you know this early morning this first day of summer
As soon as he turned that key
All the spark
All the combustion
Would reveal his own North Star?
The cruiser's "whoop-whoop" makes him jump
Alert and tense as a cattle dog he turns his head to the right
     waiting for his next signal
"You're doing just fine, son"
The trooper stands beside the open window belt buckle at
     eye level
A long look is given to the driver then the seasoned version
     beside him
"Well, that explains it"
And with a warning that stifles a chuckle, he waves the car on:
"Try to stay t' this side of the yellow line"
This young man
Shoulders broader somehow now taller without hesitation
     without instruction
Glances in the rearview
Touches the gas
And proclaims

"That was the best!"

—Ana Burtnett, Worcester

Karen Carpenter

I had this crazy dream. This lovely crazy dream.
And Karen Carpenter was there.

She was lying on the ground. I tried to speak but not a sound.
And Karen had white roses in her hair.

> She sang to me:
> "I am watching over the ladies, I know you all mean right!
> Keep the flowers in your hair, girl, and get back on your
>   feet tonight."

I could not believe my eyes, as her body began to rise,
Her eyes were bright, her arms were strong.

Now my body began to dance. The whole world was in a trance.
In her face I saw that we belonged.

> She sang to me:
> "I am watching over the ladies. We don't have to fight.
> Keep your head up, tears are fine, girl. Just get back up
>   your feet tonight."

> But Karen, we know what it's all about.
> And Karen, you know we gotta talk it out.

I had this crazy dream. This lovely, crazy dream.
And Karen Carpenter was there.

—Jolynda Burton, Montpelier

Wednesday, 2:00, Physical Therapy:
Between Exercises, Bobble Your Head

I bobble and bobble. Like St. Christopher on my dash thirty years
ago. The old rusted Mercury Capri. Journey or destination? The
demoted saint. Key stuck in the ignition. My head feels ridiculous.
Chin down, ears back. But my poor dear spine is straining to see
what's coming.

First car I'd owned myself: the old yellow Capri. After the divorce.
Wouldn't lock, but no one stole it, lost its muffler crossing the
Winooski Bridge. Even then, my neck craning, fighting the chin.
The ache to *know*. And now, that future is *now*, the past nodding
and shaking.

—*Sue D. Burton, Burlington*

Sister Stars

They dwelt. In Slavic Skies. Three. Sister Stars.
To guard. Starry Dog. Their Divine. Duty. Starry Dog
    Tied. By Iron Chains. To Little Bear.
Self-appointed. Keepers of Story. Warn: When these
    Chains break, so ends Our World.
Sibling Stars. Watch. Their. Human Sisters.
Less desired. At birth. Traded. In marriage. Planted. With
    babes. Torn. Open. And spilling.
In Labor. Denied. Lettered learning. Allowed. Anemic lives.
They watch. Their Human. Sisters. And wonder. Whose
    Our World are We guarding???"

There Is. A buzz. In Those Heavens. Talk. Of a New
    World. In need. Of New Gods.
Pilgrims. Of each. Land. Devotees. Of each. Myth. Find.
    Their Way. Remade. By New Wilds.
These Celestial. Sisters. Release. Those. Flat skies. Of man-
    made. Myth.
They seek. Fertile Wombs. Of Three. Sister Pilgrims. Plant.
    Themselves. Inside.
Weave. Female. Forms. In Which. To Grow. As New
    Women. In a New World.

These Sisters. Zorya. Dwell. There. Still.

Leaving. Starry Dog. Now. Unchained. In His Heaven.
Little Bear. Dance.

They choose. This Unknowable. And Their. Gifted Hands.
Shape. This. New World.

They. Do. Divine. Work. Spinning and Stitching. Mending
and Adorning. Their. New World.

Morn Zorya. Wakes. Their Sun. Spins. Her Rays. Into
Gleaming. Threaded Daylight.

Eve Zorya. Her Moonlit Bonnet. Bright. Weaves.
Moonglow Cloth. To Blanket. Night. Skies.

Midnight Zorya. Embroiders. Names. Of Their Dead. And
Dying. Quilts. Of Human Story. Of

ALL Story.

And so. They imagine. This New World. And so. It Is.
Dreamt. Into Being. By Stars.

—*Patricia Louise Joi Canada, Barre*

Everyone has Written a Poem About
a Winter's Night

Tonight, the fog was at once heavy enough it formed a halo
　　around the street lamp
and light enough that I could barely feel it on my face.

The sidewalks had the sheerest coating of ice, barely visible—
that meant walking was slow
and I had to be watchful,
no time to look at the winter silhouettes of the unleaved trees.

I made my way home from the theater having just seen a film
　　about America's creation
and use of the hydrogen bomb and the internal explosion in
　　the man responsible,
the dissonance between the scientist and the human.

How I wanted you there with me, probably not to talk about
　　the movie,
or for you to even reassure me that everything would be okay
between us, this disturbed country we live in, or even the future.

No, just to hold your hand would be enough for tonight.

—*Kathleen Casserly, Montpelier*

"Be Your Own Boss"

A terrible idea, seductive but silly,
at least for me, a decent man but prone
to dither and overthink, until trouble
sprouts and possibility leaves town.

Long blessed by strong women bosses,
I pine now for the muses. Don't leave
me unattended. I can't be trusted
here alone. My own devices pale.

Without you my days yawn; my leaves wilt,
my streams run dry; my streets are hot
with clamor. Boss me, ladies, please.
Clap and I'll hear water, air, their song.

I know you're here somewhere. I'm all
eyes for your beck, all ears for your call.

—*Dave Cavanagh, Burlington*
from *Please Hold*, forthcoming from Salmon Poetry

On Finding Old Age Unfathomable

The old woman who is and isn't me lifts a stick
from the mud in America and calls the shape she has drawn
her mother. It's me, says the continent. It's me,
says the girl who was and wasn't me. You're wrong,
says the woman. There's no mud in my thinking.
Come here, says the girl. There's a house you can enter
but only in a dream, hallway after hallway on your knees.
I'm looking for the samovar, says my mother. I gave it away,
I tell her, and on the spot, my old Dostoyevsky, the one
with the mosaic of sadness on the cover that I loved so much
in high school, crumbles like a cough in the unquiet air.
Which continent are we on, asks my mother. Both, I tell her,
each vast and snowy and smelling of hemlock, of thyme
and the ingredients of a thick, starchy soup. I step toward her
but a rock at the bottom slips out from my foot and I'm head down
in the dirt like a buried spoon. Histrionics, rumbles my mother.
I miss you, I say. You forgive me, she asks? A lot, but then
it starts up again, I say. And her, she nods at the girl,
have you abandoned her? It's not her, I say, that's the problem.
It's the twenty-year-old, and the thirty. They don't dare
show their faces. Maybe, says the girl, you're not looking.
Well, says the old woman who is and isn't me, maybe
you should stick to your sandbox. Remind me, I say
I've forgotten the words you were singing to your teapot.

—*Judith Chalmer, Burlington*
previously published in *3rd Wednesday*, Winter 2024

By the light of winter

The kindness of strangers—
Waiting, stopping, opening,
To the life that comes
Of its own being; mystery
Like a child's laugh which
Bubbles forth unseen
From depths, springs among
Dry life-hardened rock
To nourish the living,
To comfort the dying
Like winter's fire, red
Tongues speak to grey hands,
And ears blue and stuffed
With thought until the force
Of silence itself gives
Attention to what is
Overlooked, lost, gone,
Forgotten, ignored, and
Empty as a beggar's cup
That now opens, ready to receive.

—*Samuel L. Chambers, Essex Junction*

December 5th

found poem: source text: Why We Broke Up, *Daniel Handler*

December fifth
Our two month anniversary
I am alone.
Me in the empty getting smaller
Every Word I write to you I shouldn't have said
You read every word
How long does it stay in your head
You're not in the picture
It'll never fade, a joy
I looked us over
It's not love, what I saw, I looked
Photographs crooked
Bright red walls crumbling peeling paint
It's not something
It's so far from us

—*Shianne Charette, Cabot*

It's Poetry Month

It's poetry month and I want to join in
So I looked on the internet to see where to begin
Oh my sake and my stars it's all so confusing
The names they have for different types of poems
It all makes no sense to me
Ain't a Ballad a song
And a Blackout's when the lectric goes out
Elergy and Epitaph is something at the church
Epics go on for pages and pages, it's too many words
Concrete is what you pour for a cellar
Echo verse, Blank verse how can that work
And Diminish verse, does that mean it gets littler and littler
And I know ain't nothing free so what's up with Free verse
A Sonnet's bout love and I'd be embarrassed
Isn't a Villanelle the name of some gal on TV
I can't even saw Acrostic, Sestina
Or El-el-e-phant-ass-tic
I'm getting too old to learn all this stuff
So before I make a fool of myself
I guess I'll give up and go watch that Vilanelle gal on TV

—Mary Cheyne, Chelsea

The Comfort of a Gray Day

I am the first to admit that I love
the exuberant brilliance of a bluebird day.
Cloudless and shimmering and screaming out "Carpe Diem"—
so much to enjoy!
But my kindred spirit lies in the sleepy,
unassuming presence a gray day;
the sheer acceptance of me, to just be me,
with no pretense, no expectations.
The ability to breathe deeply and slowly
into the nurturing blanket of grayness.
Tears of grief flow freely, muscles filled with tension and anxiety
let go and release. The curtain enveloping the earth gives me
a sense of protection and security.
My innate need to DO something, or accomplish something wanes,
allowing me to be more present in the moment and
more keenly attuned to my senses and needs.
I allow myself to contemplate my life and
forgive myself for the errors I have made and
that I will continue to make, again and again,
without judgment or penalty. Just being is enough.
Gratitude for being and the simplicity of the grayness
surrounding me spreads a warmth
throughout my soul and body.

—Susan Chickering, East Montpelier

February 9, 2023

As I step out of the library,
soft coo-cooing brushes my ears

Oh, a mourning dove—
We must be nearing spring!

Searching for the sound,
I walk across to the cemetery,
where high atop an obelisk

sits the statue of a dove:

reaching across the border
from winter to spring
tiny rope tossed
bridges
death to life
heaven to earth
I almost missed it
secret message from Mom

—Alice Christian, Colchester

Stuck in a Good Book

You may call me a teacher's pet,
A book worm, ya! That's what, I bet.
I just can't help myself; I'm stuck in a good book.
It's really funny, why don't you take a look!

—Lexi Clarfeld, age 8, Colchester

Dream in the Wilderness: John Clarke Barker, 1851

Wandering into a settlement by the great falls
What is this place where the rainbows shine through the water mist?
Such a gamey smell of mutton stew simmering—am I dreaming?
As I awake with that prickly feeling
When a horsehair comes through the mattress cover
Mutton for breakfast washed down with overly fermented
Beer brought up from the basement
Temperance movement has not gotten here yet!
With the rough cracked wooden spoon, I slurp up the last of
the stew
Today is my 18th birthday and the world is wild and open
Last night, savoring the strawberry shortcake as I sat at the
wooden table
I read by the soft glowing light of the beeswax candle
Of what wonders I might see through the shimmery glass window
of the lodge
And here it is just past dawn
With this mighty falls from the north thundering down just beyond
Sweet lilac smell as I stand at the sink by the open window—am
I dreaming?
Smooth texture of the door knob being turned
Peaceful sleep under the wool blanket on a chilly night...

I awaken so hungry and cold in the woods—now I am not
dreaming
There is the falls, but no lodge, no mutton, no beer, no
strawberries...

—Peter L. Clark, Woodbury

Singer at the Well of Souls

Womb of stars filled with potentiality,
Light travels eons and creation unfolds,
Beauty and majesty in view, consciousness behind felt by some
    but not seen.

On another layer of reality, the spirit of the nebula is
    birthing creation…
She sings a power that is purple, aqua, magenta,
A melody rhythm harmony pulse,
Wave upon wave of sonic calling,
Differentiating bright glowing lights from the Well,
Each like a sunrise, a star birth, a brilliant globe of possible.
In collaboration with the Creator of all,
Her voice rises and falls, undulating with melodies not heard
    in the physical realm,
In response, one by one, or in geometric groups, nascent
    points of light
Soar forth from the crucible of conception,
Gaining definition as they emerge with multi-colored
    patterns of
Fractal complexity shining a code of essence embedded with
Gifts awaiting to spring forth,
As spirit comes into matter:
An electric magnetic mesmerizing dance of the
Manifestation of the miraculous.

—Peter Clark, Woodbury

Daytime

Hi resting brain, how are you doing today?
I need more time in bed to be more
rested.

I am tired of being talked to like I know nothing.

I am tired of having a bad problem with the people in the
world.

I am tired of looking like a problem.

I am trapped in my daytime brain most of the time.
My resting brain is nowhere to be found in the daytime.

My resting brain is asleep in the daytime like a nocturnal
creature.

My daytime self is masking the truth.
I am more than what you see.

—Conor Isaiah Cleveland, Williamstown

The Champlain Sea

after Jim Sardonis, Reverence (Whales Tails), *1989*

Sea—birthplace of all the slippery creatures,
Air—open-space filling new lungs with fresh,
Ground—wherein all before us rests.

A four-legged cousin crawled from the water,
laid out on its edge to dry and breathe deeply,
resting on its back-fins, now called feet.

Today, in green haze Vermonters call summer,
along the black tongue of the interstate, I climb
a hillock crowned with two gray granite tails—

fluked, broad, remaining parts of diving whales
caught mid-motion, burrowing back in time.
When I walk, pressing full weight onto ground,

I feel a pushback from underneath—fossil ferns,
trilobites, monsters, and mostly outspread palms
of all my dead supporting me.

—*PH Coleman, South Burlington*

velvet curtains

I had to speak about the arts—
not that the audience knew I was speaking about the arts,
but I was and I needed you to be there.

So, just before walking to the center of the room
I stepped back against the deep sill of the forty-foot-high
    window
and reached for the heavy velvet curtains.

I imagined them to be, not curtains, but rather,
the hem of your jacket—as if you were standing there
ready to accept the weight of my worry if I leaned into you.
I felt the pressure of you, urging me to stand,
once again, on my own gently coaxing me up and away.
I gathered my notes and walked forward,
said your name, and told of your dream.

I spoke to those who would listen and to those who refused.

And I thought of Dylan Thomas, Robert Frost, Harper Lee,
Hayden Carruth, Andre Dubus, Kurt Vonnegut, and you,
and how important, how essential it is to speak about the arts
as if they matter, because, like velvet curtains in a stately house,

they do.

—Mary L. Collins, Lake Elmore

The Act of Love

Your face is all I see above me,
El Greco-gaunt and taut,
your eyes sharp as spears,
brown obsidian.

I, not taut at all,
melt into the horizontal plane,
pooled, hot salted butterscotch.

You subside as I regain solidity.
Murmuring random thoughts that bind us
close as our clasped hands,
we inhale in each other's breath,
settle, rest.

—Ann Cooper, Middlebury

Nigh the Waters

April North
In the quickening, before the rush,
as sugar maples barely blush
beside the stalwart evergreen,
her catekin gold revives the scene
in view along the mountain vale—
The tender season's brightening pale.

~

Babylonica
Willow, Willow, do you weep?
Do yet your trailing tresses keep
storied secrets, whispered shame,
the weight of our ancestral blame?

Willow tree in fresh lament,
children cry, blood newly spent.
Psalms of sorrow, babies dashed—
The anguished—and the unabashed.

~

Counter-Vale
Or are your boughs a form of paise,
unlike those kin with arms upraised—
Not mourning but humility,
should such a thing concern a tree.

~

Paradoxica
Willow, Willow waking now, tell us what you know,
you, among the first to leave, and the last to go.

—*Linda Corelia, Montpelier*

hearing the phoebe: Five Haiku for the Year

on my porch swing
 —good day
 —bad day

                swatting
                at mosquitoes
                my neighbor waves back

home
her gray strands
woven in the thrush's nest

                hearing the phoebe
                now I can plan
                all my day

growing and growing
in late August
the shelf of pickles

—*Nichael Cramer, Guilford*

previously published, respectively, in *bottle rockets* #50; *Heron's Nest*, vol. XXV no. 3; the anthology *Bird Whistle*; *tiny words*, 32.1; *New England Letters* no.142

Ledger

This body is a container
for a certain number
of breaths, a certain
number of kisses.
The horizon of your skin
makes gravity a myth,
releases every trace
of music stored in my muscles.
One day all my thoughts
will narrow to those
I had in the womb,
the world's vast
nomenclature stripped
down to basic human need.
I know it's probably
written on air, but
somewhere there's a ledger
that tells us
how much of our breath
we've given to dispute,
how much to song.
Remind me again
how not to be
a howl on a string.

—*Stephen Cramer, Burlington*
forthcoming in *Hole in the Head Review*

Sunflower

"Joy is not made to be a crumb,"
Mary Oliver once wrote, but isn't that
how it often shows up at first? One crumb
of attention, then another, and another
until you're able to follow the trail
leading to the volunteer sunflower
you hadn't noticed blooming by the garden.
"Volunteer," we say, meaning no human
hand nestled that seed in the ground,
though the same could be said of joy too,
which seems to spring up out of nowhere
when you see the face of the flower
the French call *tournesol*, meaning
"turned toward the sun." And don't we
each carry a small sun in our chests
that tells us where to turn, where it's warm,
where something bright has struggled up
out of the earth, and is now calling your name?

—James Crews, Shaftsbury

Slip Away

for Wes Howe, 3/28/87–12/03/21

I heard more people are dying from overdoses than car crashes.
And not because we're driving less or cars are safer.
There was joy in driving a little too fast when we were young and
    fresh out.
Highschool weekends driving around loose gravel roads looking
For something to do. Perfect weather. Perfect summers,
    snowy winters.
Showing off for a girl was more likely to kill you than being
    broken,
Camped out, traveling, sliding some sorry needle into your arm.
I heard the streets are flooded with smack, "that grabs a hold of
    you and won't
Let go," My lover said a few months after I found him nodded
    out, drooling in his car with a spoon on the dash.
Occasionally he would surface like a fish to speak the truth.
    Before he
slipped the hook and descended into the murky lake of lies.
    I tried to hold him.
I read a clutch of novels, listened to folks talk on the radio,
    visited places
I went with him. I heard his folks tell me that he loved me
    rather than blame me.
I told my story and most everyone I know has lost someone now.
As storms flood the land or the devastating heat, we all grow
    unsettled.
They slip away and we lose them. It never ends.

—Jezebel Crow, Woodbury

Winter Apple Trees

Apples hanging from the branches
Having survived the long winter
As
Petrified vessels of ice cider
Like a cask on a St Bernard.

Cedar wax wings fly in and out of the branches
Pecking away at the red globes
As
Shreds of apples drop onto the melting snow below
Like confetti celebrating the end of winter.

Trees dropping the fruits from fall and winter
Making way for the blossoms of spring
As
The deer enjoy these treats
Like an appetizer before the grand feast of summer.

—*Terri Crowther, Washington*

The Juniata's waters

The Juniata's waters are high, and the dog runs far
ahead of us, clearly engaged in sniffing out the awakening
groundhogs. Here is the first forsythia in full bloom I've
seen this season. We each have a small umbrella to
ward off the occasional raindrops that we can see making
linked rings on the river's silken surface. As we walk
you put out your hand, and I take it in
mine. I am about to say I love you when
you point across the water, and I see the slow
beating of a heron's wings, making for the opposite shore.

—*Ralph Culver, South Burlington*
previously published in *The Winter Window*, Winter 2023

I heard you were back

I looked for you at the Villa Nova,
but it changed its name to the Governor's Pub,
then burned down. I looked for you, parked
with some local boy on the backroads of town,
but there are streetlights and houses and public
in all the old, best places. I looked for you
at the Mini mart, loitering in front of the girlie
magazines and trying to buy beer or watching
one of the older boys buy it for you. I stood
out in the Bowling Alley parking lot.
I thought maybe I'd see your car go by.
I went as far as Bethel—all crunchy now
with boutiques and frozen yogurt.
I looked for you in all the places I remembered.

—*Douglas K. Currier, Winooski*

Diminished

We are all so much less now:

Climate refugees from the Cree Nation
of Old Nemaska, up in smoke...

Iraqi farmers from Basra,
a former bread basket, gone dry....

Even Vermonters have been flooded,
mucked by muddied waters,
torn asunder, gutted houses, ruined crops.

Soon we will ally with polar bears,
beached pilot whales,
and sky-filled
wing-flapped
shadows
of
carrier pigeons.

—*daithí, Montpelier*

What if Grocery Store

No moon, dark, dark, driving rain, the doors beckoned
    bright as Florida sunshine, pushing my way
through, I didn't have a list. Sometimes I just like to look at
    what's on all the shelves.

Rounding a corner, surprised to see him standing there,
    looking at beer brands I hadn't seen
since 1972, he went well before the craft beer phase. Nice
    to see him in one piece, not like his last
moments in ICU before they turned all the machines off.
    He didn't see me pass by.

In the wine aisle now, I love the bottle names, of course she
    was there. She's clutching a bottle
of Harvey's Bristol Creme, that smile with the gap between
    your front teeth, I knew it well. She
wasn't much of a cook but she had a firm belief that sherry
    could fix any dish she tried to make.

Up another aisle, I see her looking at the shelves with all
    the past date items checking out the pies,
dressed as usual in pearls, and a mink stole. If I stood with
    her on a corner in New York City,
in minutes a taxi would pull over to pick us up. Never
    understood why she brought those pies
to Thanksgiving, maybe to drive her daughter crazy.

Down another aisle I almost ran into the old lady pushing a
     cart piled high with diapers and infant
formula. A little baby in the seat, was cradling another in
     her arms. She stood out dressed in a sari
with a blue stripe, head covered, sandals on weathered feet.
     Kolkata is far from here.

I saw him go into the men's room, dressed in a blue linen
     suit. He spent a lot of time in bathrooms,
a stomach wrecked by booze and anxiety. He left secrets
     behind, the War gave him a lifetime of
nightmares.

I heard the gun go off but no way was I going in that aisle. I
     always wanted to save him.

In the bread aisle there she was, back in her prime,
     babushka on her head, wearing those shoes
that hurt her feet. Purse on one arm, hands squeezing the
     Wonder Bread. She loved that stuff,
sang its praises, I always thought it was inedible.

Enough for one night, I headed out the door pulling my
     coat tight against the rain and the wind.

—W. Dall, Montpelier

Ancient Oak

Withstanding time, you endure
blizzards, hurricanes, flash floods,
and raging fires.

Heavily you lean, bark rough
and scarred.

Limbs reach for the sky,
spew secrets of what you know.

Gracefully you age,
nourishing new growth.

You have become more beautiful,
and stronger, from such a little sprout.

—*Corinne Davis, Montpelier*

Kindred Solitude

Frost crystallizes on glass
creating an illusion,
a prison of ice.
We seek the sanctity
of shelter
but harness the restless
desire for kindred spirits
in a void of
Bitter Cold.

Frost burdened nights;
a refuge and an isolation.
Does the ice create the illusion?
Or does it give reality legs
on which to run through our
minds, driving us mad?
On the darkest days
when even the moon hides
behind clouds,
a weary soul asks
for another,
unhindered by winter's
expectations.

—*Sarah E. DeBouter, Berlin*

A Promise for Spring

I think of you and
the world turns
green green green

Surely there is such a thing
as too much abundance:

Ivy that races over the thawing earth,
a wildfire that continues
to grow and
a body that doesn't know
when to stop.

But there is no fire, is there?
And since when does abundance have
to be something good?

The long awaited flowers of spring
will bloom and
rot before
I see you again,

You,
You who knows only how to take.

—*Grace Decker, Burlington*
previously published in the *Gist*, Fall 2023

To Our Indolent Cancer

Ah, our lazy, our listless, our lovely, our lingering
languid turtle; mooching, smooching slow dancer;
dozy, dossing, easygoing footdragger; tinkering,
plod-plodding procrastinator; incipient necromancer;
lackadaisical, lackluster, loafing, lagging lug;
watched pot; fainéant of fainéants; otiose slug;

our break-taking, oscitant artisan slacker; our unfussed,
watching-the-grass-grow dawdler; our most phlegmatic
sloth; maundering, moony-loony manatee; nonplussed,
relaxed, dilatory, shell-slumbering snail; our aesthetic,
asthenic, torpid tortoise; lumbering Laodicean; dillydally-
ing, desultory lol-lol-lollygagger; our shillyshallshally;

our dear-there-where cancer, hear our lull-lull-lullaby.
You can, sir, be kind, be gentle, be easy, no need to rush.
We still have loads, bags, oodles of time. Remember: I die,
you die. We're both here now, why the sudden push?

—*Greg Delanty, Burlington*
previously published in the *New York Review of Books*, December 21, 2023

The Anthropocene, Montpelier Vermont

A new line on the time scale
A new line on the buildings of main street
Written in mud, written in debris, written in water

I watch a woman approach that line on East State street
Wearing a blank stare, wearing a blue bathing suit
"Going for a swim?"
My ears fill with every working fire alarm in town
My nostrils fill with the stench of septic and petroleum
"Maybe" she says looking straight ahead
Approaching the intersection that
Has become a new branch of the river

A new line growing up her body as it disappears into the
      caustic water
A new line on the buildings of main street
Showing where the waters crested this time

—nd dentico, East Montpelier

Pruning the Apple Trees

I trim the deer-damaged branches,
and the limbs that cross other limbs.
I lop off skyward sucker shoots,
to let more light penetrate the foliage.
The results are drastic.

We feel the throb of our own losses,
the pain of every phantom limb,
the lingering of love.
Do the trimmed trees ache?
Will there be fruit this fall?

—Deborah Dickerson, Bristol

Apricity

spark of winter sun
ignited snowscape delight
prisms riotous

—*Monica DiGiovanni, Montpelier*

July 4th, 2023

The peepers, bullfrogs sing
their chaotic chorus,
hubris in high grass
sky pink teases billowing clouds
a mock mountain scape over the misty hills.
Low rumble of thunder,
zig-zag shock of lightening
then all this becomes a stage-set
for unfurling flowers of light
that dazzle
and we, silent before the spectacle
are agape at what humans have wrought.
But then a different thought—
of wars fought centuries past
and right now "over there"
rockets red glare, bombs bursting in air
bringers of death, smell of burning flesh.

Yet along this hillside ledge
summer life calls out.
Booming, fire, smoke—
crickets, peepers are not impressed.

—*Arlene Iris Distler, Brattleboro*

What Remains

Gratitude in the hour of anguish
Blessings when misery seems all around.
Spirits drained and lost.
Broken lines, words, thoughts
Rhythm and rhyme won't fit.
Another post, questions
Have you felt it yet?

Thank you anyway, my Creator.
I'm furious at each imprisoned hope.
Each murdered dream,
Thank you for my rage.
And the bruises of what remains.
Abrasions deep and bloodied dreams
Thank you for the last remaining thing.
I'll take the hope and I'll raise it too.
Because despite it all,
I still believe in You.

—*Mariessa Dobrick, Barre*

Inheritance

Underneath the rough-ridged exterior of a butternut shell
I notice the soft glow from the golden-brown folds within
And I am reminded of the greatest inheritance I have or can pass on.

Beyond classification, a simple folk appreciation
For the wonders of the natural world,
Especially in this blessed part of it known as Vermont.

I feel this vernacular of nature better than I can speak it.

Contentment and vague yearning
At the sight of moss-covered stones.

Reverence beneath a massive old oak,
Perhaps just a sapling when my great-grandparents wed
On this chapel of land eighty years ago.

Gratitude upon finding the feather of a falcon
From a peregrine species that humans nearly destroyed—
But then helped bring back.

May future generations know themselves to be
The descendants of this kinship with nature,
Bound by a chord of humility, awe, and responsibility.

—*Jared Duval, Montpelier*

It Is the Light

It is the light that defines our days
Shafts unexpectedly slice the forest floor
Revealing deep-rooted mystery
Fuchsia shadowed mountainsides
Face us majestically
Declaring their permanence
Amber iridescent gold
Fills faces on summer afternoons
We wonder and wander
Questioning our fragile
Humanity

—*Maggie Eaton, East Montpelier*

Jelly Donut

He liked those the best
And crullers.
Small nuggets
Of joy.
I just retrieved
A good memory.
And I choose
To cherish it.

—*Kathryn Eberly, Montpelier*

A Trick of the Light Miraculous

A droplet bent within a band and
                 faced the sun
The sun sang orange and yellow
Chanting backwards from seven to one
Each note arced a separate, yet blended band
Seven arcs for seven notes
                 in tones bright or mellow
The droplet—one of trillions in the band—
                 thinly echoed
Train your eyes upon this fading line
                 before I die
But no *one I* could e'er have spoken
Bent and thin before it faded
Farewell, sang no one
                 to no one there,
Goodbye, bygone indigo

—*Krikmöklet Egelanaard, Chelsea*

The Catch

Love is oft a virtued bird
In flight, alone, and soaring free
Rarely 'tis found a fish floundered
Swimming in school through a salty sea

But perhaps this fish spots an anxious worm
And swallows him whole too quick to taste
Then yanked from the class to which 'twas born
To become some fisherman's prize or bait

—*Nietzsche Danann Egelanaard, Chelsea*

Be By Myself

I brush my teeth by myself.
I sleep by myself.

—*Ezra, age 3, Colchester*

December storm

Tonite is a night of regrets
the ghosts of my past haunt me
like the stormy night (showstorm) sky snow
why now, always 3 am
the time of the wolves as my brother says.
Another of the ones that mildly haunt regrets.
Outside the trees silently grow,
those oldest poets , words of bark and bud
wood yearly verse prose
they take the long view
a lot there to learn,

all around the tales of technology distract and annoy,
car lights, water pumps, fridges hum
the distant glow from the hospital
the neon green from a neighbor who needs to be seen,
that thief who stole the darkness
the too bright porch lights from the scared
always trying to bring conclusions to stories
before the end that hasn't come yet
witty , ha
enough for now

—*buzz ferver, Berlin*

A Drink of Field

summer holds the land at perfect sensory level—
fresh-cut hay simmers in rectangular pans
rake tines scratch earth's bumpy scalp
dirt dust and sun-caked loam
release soft into the air—
the field hovers
in a heat-hazed soil mirage
leaving granules on the corners of lips
balls of feet, silted fingertips
drinking in the season's scent
balanced on the bent backs
of timothy and clover
whose crushed purple cheeks
perfume the heated grass
fodder for four-stomached cows
and all those others
who hunger

—*Ann Fisher, Lincoln*

The Connecticut

We're drawn to rivers — lifeblood of the land,
mirror of the sky, *mater aquae*. Rivers
give rise to poetry, mythos — the hand
of the Almighty carves these valleys, gives
us sustenance and stories and love, or
maybe the river is wisdom, or time,
or a fictional forever. Ignore
the river at your peril — it knows.

                                                          I'm
thinking of this river — the Abenaki
named it for what they knew to be true,
Kwenitekw, the Long River of talking
stones and fish of every kind, the fusion
of this world and the next. In the storms
that whip up whitecaps, in the icy strange
winter silence, in spring floods, in the warm
caress of summer, the river is change.

—*Michael Fleming, Brattleboro*

Batten Kill Through Mill Pond

By the side of a stewarded river
hugging a small town center,
a pocket of greensward lined with thicket
sits near a pond that eagerly flows
    from under the bridge toward the shelf
      of triadic forces...

Three thick sheets
transparent and sparkling
roaring and rushing
blasting down
onto the boulder plain,
which is biding its time
as the wet deluge
planes and polishes
its bald head.

On the fringe of the plain and on one foot,
fixedly peering through the thunderous
downpour, the great long-legged bird
of subtle bluish-gray stands perfectly still
    patiently...
      waiting.

—*Julia H. Fonte, Poultney*

Bones

Life takes a toll:
It steals your bones
until they're   nothing
but   weary   sticks

Wading into the unknown:
Waiting to feel something strong underneath them
                    once again.

You march into the turbulent seas
                searching for peace
                searching for something steady
to shield you

from the raging storm
                threatening to suffocate you,
                threatening to pull apart
the tendrils of your heart,   but

When there's no peace,
There's nothing left but to release
Your demons.

Have hope.

—*Elias Kai Francis, Williamstown*

Bittersweet Still Life

My grandmother, my mother's mother, had been an artist
well known for her landscapes and still life paintings,
and so the earthenware jug you see in that photo
came from her, but it was my mother's request

that sent me out into the rain again that day to cut
bittersweet for her, and the arrangement pictured
there is my Mother's. Not surprising that she
was so good at it nor that I knew exactly where

to find the old cider jug and teal cloth Grandmother
had used in so many of her still life arrangements.
I remember shaking the rain from those cuttings
before I handed them to Mother along with

her pruning shears, knowing she would edit what I had cut,
but glad to see her so engaged, so focused on trimming
dead twigs and leaves. She did choose to keep three
yellowing leaves in the center *for interest,* she said.

I watched her fuss over draping the teal cloth, and
when she finished, I shot a photo in the waning light
of that stormy afternoon. My hair and clothes still damp,
I held the camera so she could see the captured image,

the dramatic effect of storm-dark background against
foregrounded, glistening bittersweet, one crinkled,
folded leaf, flat against the white jug. She simply
nodded and lay down again. She tired easily.

It was a long illness.

—*Sarah Franklin, Montpelier*

In Trust

I'd like to go back to sailing, taken by the wind
or working with it, sometimes at a good pace,
sometimes flying, other times caught in irons
standing still and then, oh, the quiet,
but for the wind rising in
a whoosh or a whisper.

In Lightning races, I was always part of the crew,
told what to do, holding the jib like plot lines,
moving back and forth across the beam
passing under the boom, except for once, the time
I did not come around *hardily*. Still, I'd like
to go back to sailing and the days when

the captain and the crew worked together.
Moving the boat effectively is what mattered.

—*debby franzoni, Castleton*

so much more in common

yes you have blonde hair and i have black
your dog barks and mine says "quack quack"
i live in your old house and you want it back
so what do we do to get back on the track?

i'll stop rhyming for a minute
so you can catch your breath
here's a cup of tea
and a croissant
i give it to you even though
you cannot ever seem to pronounce it right

i come from far away and so do you
and today we are here
you are my neighbor because you are standing next to me
    right now
i believe in miracles
you believe in mackerels
we both like hot mushroom barley soup on a cold day

we have so much more in common than we have differences
we both want a warm place to live and good food and good
    friends
as the snow melts all around us
i notice we are both smiling
we both have wet feet
i will get dry socks for you
will you read me your new poem when i come back?

—*david fried, Montpelier*

Wake of the Flood

You came halfway across the world seeking asylum.
You'd wait on the corner and I'd pick you up, cook for you,
teach you English, hold you at night.
But the flood blocks me from coming to you,
forces you to stay in your house and move to the second floor.
I say, if it rises any higher, I will come.
You say, how could you rescue me? Do you have a boat?
I'll borrow a horse and find an alternate route across this
    war-torn country,
like the one you left, with blown-out roads.

You used to tell me, when I drove through snowstorms to see
    you, *no heroics.*
When they said, it's supposed to be bad weather, I don't
    know if you'll meet for your lesson,
I said *oh no. We'll meet.* And we did, with the power out and the
    trees down around us.

This ceaseless rain which has never stopped me before.
You say, it's so sad. We can't walk today.
You show me videos of water bubbling up on the road. Show
    me your face, I say.
We've walked together every day for two hours since we met.
Because we are so European. To stabilize us. Because we are
    health fanatics.
And the excruciating tragedy of such a simple thing: we can't
    walk today.
We can't walk in the sun.
I never appreciated it before.

Trapped inside my house, I have the sense of a nuclear
    holocaust.
I cannot protect you. I feel like I will die without you.
I would give everything I have
for one more walk with you in the sun.

—*Gaia Fried, Montpelier*

Stilt Walking

When a bubble bath isn't enough
I lie down and play Leonard Cohen on Spotify
and pray to G-d
I fall asleep and dream of walking on stilts
On a path along a lake I do not know yet
but am in love with already
My face is close to the blue and clouds and sun
I glide on my stilts and wave to friends as I pass
I ask myself what this means
Perhaps it is an answer from G-d and
Leonard and my grandparents
Who I can only see with closed eyes
Perhaps they are giving me a boost
So I can see the view and see that it is good
I can't look into a crystal ball
I can't know where decisions will take me
but I know there is a path
and I will not be alone
because they are with me
If I invite them

—*Navah Fried, South Burlington*

Judgments

Do we know what we do to others?
How cruel our actions can be!
Are we without sin? That we can judge all,
the people we hurt without a word, withdraw.

Look at ourselves.
Have we hurt others with judgments?
God accepts us all as we are.
Faults we all have.

Have we accepted our faults and tried to change?
If only in our minds, not in our hearts,
or actions, we have work to do.
It's not only me; it's you too.

—*Marcy Frink, Worcester*

Pledge

Not this for which I stand:
this madness,
this malevolence of arms,
this single finger thrust into the air.

Brought to the cliff's edge
we are taught the water's demise,
but dare not to bear witness
to the foam's bold coupling
with the broken black shore.
Always this lesson, this
same
 old
  lesson,
     and yet
I continue to want
more from two souls
united by flesh—
a pact between mortals
still scared of the dark.

It is this for which I stand,
for which I continue to dream:
to be mortal and believe,
to learn laughter between screams.

—*Jamie Gage, Stockbridge*
from *True If Destroyed*, Finishing Line Press

Blessed Life

Hard-worker, the nice nurse,
married with kids.
Happiest, saddest emotions,
loudest, quietest.
Be yourself,
be your best self everyday.
Pray, bless others,
bless yourself.
You may be living in darkness now,
but sunlight will always rise.

—*Harriet Galfetti, Berlin*

Chronic

be patient, they say
with an IV drip of erratic,
biopsy of morals,
fractures of trust,
notions of benign

try to be stable, they say
finger the pulse
hope for no relapse
be a good patient

—*Claire Gallagher, Barre*

The Afternoon Porch in the Morning

I'm coming down later than her for a change,
I'm making the coffee as usual,
When I find where she is, I know it's a warning
'Cause she's out on the afternoon porch in the morning.

There's a porch out in front, a porch out in back,
The front one faces the sun as it's setting,
But the one out in back sees the sun as it's dawning:
That's why we sit there in the morning.

We normally read, separate and silent,
The *Times* on the front in the evening;
On the porch out in back she's knitting or darning
While I read aloud every morning.

If I see her out front when we should be out back
Or I see her out back in the gloaming,
Then I know that it's meant as a silent reproach—
I must be an eel, a pig, or a roach—
She's stewing on something, I know it's a warning,
She's out on the afternoon porch in the morning.

—*Walt Garner, West Brookfield*

Breeze sighing softly
Sea grass swaying in the light
Waves caressing sand

—*Susan Gerretson, Montpelier*

passing by

if you happen
by the shore
or anywhere
(within reason of course)
look up and see them
flying high above you
walking close beside you
floating coasting landing
diving calling being standing

be sure
to tell them
the old man
that used to come
to see them
and sometimes
even feed them
won't be coming anymore

look up and they may answer
thanks for the sandwich!
what was once bound
is now free to soar

—Brian Goodwin, Middlesex

A flash flood always begins with a drop of rain on a stone*

The steady rain signaled the toads
to migrate en masse, buoyant,
though not elated
as they were in spring
with the prospect of love in the air.
Loving to come out in the rain,
preferring the dark and the wet,
they crisscrossed the dirt road,
until they silently drowned,
then were flattened,
leaving traces of themselves,
stains on the road,
barely visible,
except to me and my dog
on our daily pilgrimage.

—Andrea Gould, Plainfield
*from Uncommon Type by Tom Hanks

The Maple

I have lived
In this valley for all the
Years that my rings tell
I have seen the new buds burst and
Grow and green and fall; the ongoing cycle.
And have felt my leaves turn scarlet and drop
I have felt the birds sing in my branches though the summer.
I have seen their hatching in my hollows and their passing
For those here for one
Iota of time know I have
Seen the cycles of this
Earth come and go
Flowing like the river
Watching it from when
I was a seedling reaching
For the sun so high up
Growing an inch at a
Time until I had leaves
That sprouted and sap
That ran until I was
Ninety-nine feet tall
Growing from the roots

Here   Below

—Sara Graham, Barre

Envious Moon

Oh insecure moon,
Thou art envious of the sun's
Glitter, glamour, and glory.
You creep in front of the sun
To steal its glow.
For a brief moment, you are crowned
With a corona of light.
With your power, you
Turn day into night.
But brief is your reign.
You vanish as your shadow
Is soon swallowed by dazzling day.

—*William Graham, Stowe*

Making Paella in America

Sweet, earthy saffron permeates
shellfish in broth on the pristine stove.
Steam rises, crab and shrimp
bounce in the bubbling boil.

Nostalgia coats the pan's edge,
impregnates tomato, bell pepper,
minced garlic, then parsley.

Believing family immutable,
she labors with stubborn pride,
refusing to smooth her husband's
woundedness into healing.

She stomachs longing in a way
I cannot—beside her,
ghosts of culinary matriarchs
stir the Spanish rice.

Seafood, shelled, drapes
the yellowed rice on plate,
and all that can be heard
around the worn and wooden table
is the unbearable clicking of forks.

—Gail Grycel, Westminster West
previously published in The Poet Magazine, July 2022

Muscle memory

How much of this embrace is yours and mine
and how much is memory of mother's comfort
are all our embraces
nesting dolls of memory
adapting to new arms and then others
is this love unique
or the latest lily pad on which to float
over life's torrents
the undertow and rip
can I rest here a while?

Will you entwine me in your arms
are we us
or are we our parents
and their parents
and a history of embraces
orange light kissing roiling water
moon tickling spruce branches
dog rolling in grass by the grave
raspberries dripping off stems
the eternal love of midsummer grasses and crickets
the long light of late day
speckled heavens
cocoon of darkness?

—*Jennifer Gundy, Marshfield*

First Mud Season in Vermont

Everybody mentions it, the newscaster, of course the weather guy
mothers waiting with me to pick up their kids after school
well, somebody got stuck in the mud, dirt road
where is this dirt road? I didn't have a chance to ask, the kids
    poured out
I hear somebody's car was stuck in the mud for two days
same day he lost his job, tractor pulled it out, it was an old car
    anyway
certain roads are closed because of mud, I know it's not funny
oh and everybody wants everybody to clean up the yards
because it's mud season and the snow has melted
revealing all the trash beneath that blanket, once pristine
    and bright
and breathtaking, now gray icy spiky mounds
I got a bag and picked up around the condo: plastic, paper,
rubber, rag, cardboard, tin, glass
people are wearing sweatshirts outside, shivering
even the weather guy says it's not warm yet
I'm not wearing long johns anymore, still need hat, gloves, scarf
still scrape mud off boots, I thought I'd be finished with boots
    by now
no yellow forsythia trumpet spring's arrival yet
no purple crocuses creep in the grass yet
I saw a robin this morning, tiny hopping thing
by a strapping maple tree, standing tall
its uppermost veins fanning across the blue sky
stripped down, but not asleep, something is happening
sweep out the trash, something is happening under it all

—*N.G. Haiduck, Burlington*

The Last Man to Die for a Mistake

Vietnam Women's Memorial, Washington, DC

Bedded on sandbags, he's been gut-shot,
The femoral artery breached—he'll be gone
In ten minutes. The hand that clutches his trousers
Can't hold back the inevitable.
The nurse who cradles him sees the spirit struggling for release
From the agonized mouth. She'll do what she can to soothe him,
Record his dying words for what family there might be—
Standard procedure till the Huey lands. Her friend scans the sky
As if staring could hurry it along.
The third nurse, the one you don't see at first, kneels apart,
Shoulders slumped, one hand splayed open on her knee,
The other holding the soldier's helmet,
Staring at it as if it might hold a clue
Or as if battling to control angry tears, or at last opening herself
To the futility of it all: his wounds, her comrades' care,
The ineffectual reassurance
Of the standing nurse's hand
On the elbow of the woman holding him.
In time, this bronze will weather to olive drab,
To colors more as they were in life—
But there's no iron in it,
So you'll never see the bloodstains
On his shirt, her hands. Our hands.

—*Roberta Harold, Montpelier*

Undoing

The sun illuminates my bed. I watch the light as it
    crawls away.
Fuzzy whiteness, glowing. I breathe you in like
    electricity. Split easy.
Like melting. Like a drip, humming.
I'm sliding up.   Going.   And going.

The shade will do. With its whispers and wants. With
    its half-ness. With its
holiness.
    With its I-don't-want-to-ness. Scraping strands of
      sedation. She.
    Please, be non-specific.

Red. A hard red smear. The reek of it raw and septic.
    A stain, dark as rash,
smearing the soil of your insides. A red scarf dancing in
    the raw brittle air. Red
like hunger's screams. Pulling.
A cut-up life. A careful carving. A ripped reality.
    And night like day still
Unreliable.

That's enough now. Let the paint dry.
You can try to ignore the fumes, but the stink stays.
I said, *tell me.*   But I've changed my mind.
Here. Give it to me. It is light as smell. Empty as you want.
I know. I made it so.

—*Tracy Haught, Montpelier*

Visitors from the Permafrost

Today, on Day 8,
I finally could stand upright long enough
to scramble eggs for my kids.
I'm turning the corner! I announced,
proudly whisking with minimal wheezing.
But the headline says that,
in the permafrost of the Arctic,
human pursuits like mining and shipping
could be stirring up other viruses—
ancient ones that have been trapped in the ice
for thirty thousand years.
These pathogens could be waking up
after a long, refreshing slumber,
stretching their limbs and readying themselves
to meet us for coffee.
As I marvel at my ability
to move my body across the kitchen,
I can't help but wonder how long I will be standing
before the primordial diseases
show up at our collective doorstep,
before we throw up our hands
and let the virions feast
on our elbows and earlobes
and the tips of our tender toes.

—*Jen Heller, Montpelier*

Shelter

At home, the Buddha stone
makes peace on a birch stump,
the air streaks blue,
and all the naturals are coming up,
umbilicus into petal.

Here where night gathers
the cooing of songbirds,
a soft voice lifts from a bundle of feathers.
I'm sure she's telling someone,
didn't we have a good day,
I love you, kiss kiss.
The trees sigh and if you only breathe,
you might hear nuzzling in a nest.

And I think, oh yes,
I'll sleep out here tonight.
If death should happen by,
I'll be quiet in camouflage,
a butterwing among the stars,
impossible to see,
and harder still to catch.

—*Kathleen Herrington, Montpelier*

Skunk Diplomacy

He is dressed to the nines, in a tailcoat so fine,
yet he's hardly come ready to play.
Just a peaceable beast, on the hunt for a feast,
but we don't dare to get in his way.
For you see, even though, easy come easy go,
is his nature more often than not,
this diminutive guy, in a pinch, must rely
on the only good weapon he's got.

He works hard at his task, digging grubs in the grass,
and if somebody threatens him there,
he prefers to move on, then come back when they're gone
to resume the pursuit of his fare.
If you block his retreat, he will stomp his front feet,
while his glare warns his patience won't last.
That's his final display before wrecking your day,
so you'd better get out of there fast.

He dislikes what comes next, since it leaves him a mess
and it spoils that tuxedo he wears.
If you still won't desist, he'll release a foul spritz,
and a lesson to last you for years.

—*Sam Hewitt, Essex Junction*

Wandering sorrow

after Yeats, "The Song of Wandering Aengus"

Killing is a form of our wandering sorrow...
                    —*Rilke,* Sonnets to Orpheus, *2.11*

Remember Aengus, fresh hazel, berries
ripening like lovers on the green vine.

You have never seen hazel or berries.

Oil from Arabia in barrels
sent to China, plasticized, red as cherries,
slips thin between your soles and burning sand.
You walk toward small ships, bobbing like cherries
in a bucket on a kitchen table.

When the boat sinks in the blue Aegean—
folded paper in a London puddle—
your mother mourns, even as another
soul appears, another voice to reason
that wandering human tides are fungible;
some are better off, and some must suffer.

—*Cindy Ellen Hill, Middlebury*
from *Love in a Time of Climate Change,* forthcoming from Finishing Line Press

Winter's Song

Chickadee dee dee dee
Chickadee dee dee dee
I love you!
Small fearless and faithful
You stay the winter
As green mountain tops turn white
And southbounders high tail it outta here
Your black capped crown and
Grey white racing stripes create
Symmetry on snowy landscapes
Belly and back feathers white as snow
Keep you hidden from hungry owls
You and your musical flock bring
Joy and entertainment
Your steadfast energy sustains
All the way to spring as daffodil
Shoots withstand the blasts of March
It's a delight to sing Winter's song with you
Chickadee dee dee dee
Chickadee dee dee dee dee

—*Alicia Hingston, Danville*

If

If I were a musician
I would write birdsong
    play it from treetops
and the eaves of tall buildings
Draw the sheltered onto their porches

Everyone would pause
    lay down their phones
their books   their spatulas
    look to the skies
searching for the voice
they once had

—*Lily Hinrichsen, Bristol*

Back to the Sea

Sand sitting
and sketching
the guy sitting
under a sun
blocking orange
umbrella over
the wood blue
Appalachian
big old chair.

—*Linda Hogan, Montpelier*

Sew and Tell

The treadle, the foot on the treadle,
working together to stitch fabric
into a day dress that will see
many travels. The towns and
the people in it near and far
set the stage for long ago
wanderlust and swirling
memories of taffeta and
warm sun and cool soda pop.
She sits in her recliner and
remembers the up and down
sound of the needle in threaded
pressure foot stitching together
the fabric of a colorful life.

—Linda Hogan, Montpelier

Halfway in Between

with a nod to A.A. Milne

I've an in between dog
And an in between cat.
Wherever they are that's not where it's at.

They're halfway in
And they're halfway out.
They sit in the window pretending to pout.

They're halfway in the cupboard
And halfway in the den.
Their tails are in the open and their heads are in the pen.

They're halfway up the stairs
And they're halfway down.
They've half a smile and half a frown.

They're halfway in the garden
And halfway in the path.
And when it's time to bathe they get halfway in the bath.

They're halfway in the window
And halfway in the door.
They're halfway on the carpet and halfway on the floor.

They're half awake
And they're halfway dozed.
With eyes half open and eyes half closed.

Frankly, I can't get it through my head.
They aren't quite here and they aren't quite there.
They aren't really anywhere.
They're somewhere else instead.

—*Jim Hogue, Graniteville*

When It Rains in January, Go to the Movies

Find the cashier on her knees restocking
the Chuckles. It's both plea and prayer. *Buy some.*
If only for that red taste of walking
to Snows' corner store, your daddy's loose change
filling the tight pocket of your acid-
washed jeans, and how it seemed that everything
might last—VHS tapes, New Coke, techno,
crimped hair, Michael Jackson and Day-Glo and

love. It all tastes so artificial now.
And cruel. So let yourself cry. No one's
here but the actor who's left his only
son, the leading lady on lithium, and
you with all this sweet loss on your tongue like
some glorious sugar-crusted jewel.

—*Michelle Fay Holder, Montpelier*

Ghost Dance

I have no idea
why the frog would have left
his swamp to hop over

the dirt road
to the barren field beyond,
but, flattened by a car,

his form slowly melded
with the gravel,
until one morning,

he was the pale lacey
last version of his shape
and I imagined

how, like the Northern Paiutes,
this was his ghost dance,
imploring the spirits of

his amphibian forbearers
to help him cross over—
a comfort, even in his failure.

—*Sarah Hooker, Marshfield*

Long Distance Love

A friend sends
A picture of three chickens
Standing in a kind of
Formation
On a road where
The snow has begun
To retreat.
Funny, I tell her
I was humming the theme from
Green Acres last evening
And thinking about people
Who move to rural places
In search of serenity
While also yearning
For a Trader Joe's.
As for myself
I remain smitten with
Mountains
Majestic but
Unpretentious
And the way
Rural silence calms me
Like Miles Davis playing
A ballad.
A serenity
My friend says he finds
in the ever changing
Sky.

—*Reuben Jackson (1956–2024), Vermonter at Heart*
from a forthcoming poetry volume published by Rootstock Publishing in 2024

Comprehend

found poem: source text: eaarth, *Bill McKibben*

Starting to comprehend glaciers melt
Enormous oil fields, gas wells killing trees
Industrial generations increases water
Dwindling fossil fuel
Depriving energy
Farmworkers marched blowing dust
Warmer orchard trees die starvation

—*Jacob, Cabot*

Beekeeping

Once, we kept bees, in hives—
or, *they* kept *us*, kept us mesmerized,
kept us drunk on dandelions,
dazed and dizzy by roadsides,
kept us spellbound in fields
dusted in pollen, all abuzz,
kept us out in those downpours
in petals humming in orchards,
kept us fed on ambrosia,
appetites aroused—the bees, the bees
left us amazed under plum trees.

—Mary Elder Jacobsen, North Calais
from *Stonechat*, Rootstock Publishing

Searching for the Light

The light has faded on this winter evening.
Fresh snow blankets the yard.
Having coaxed my son into snow pants, boots, mittens, and
    a coat,
We set out to play.

I had not noticed the head lamp clasped in his small hands
but now it is in the air
and now it plunges deeply
into the pile of white flakes.

His laughter rings out.
The game goes on.
The light tossed and then buried.
Small, mittened hands digging and retrieving.

So often have I searched for the missing light.
A child's game reminds me—
The light that is buried can yet be found.

—Joan Javier-Duval, Montpelier

Crown Our Tomorrows

freckles
like checkers

i'll be the
b r o w n

the little king
announces

as he knocks
repeatedly ...

not waiting
for answer.

through t h e
checkerboard

glass of my
side d o o r

he sees me,
bursts in with

EXCITE-
MENT &

six year-old
confidence.

yesterday
we t i e d

... s o   i t' s
rematch day.

—*Anna N. Jennings,*
West Townsend

Freya

sweet, joy
nice, cozy
comfortable
happy
soft ears
warm
Freya dog

—Malachi Johns, age 9, Roxbury

Sledding

Sledding on crunchy snow
Joyful scream, crash and tumble
Race to the bottom, excited laughter

Crunch, shooo, woosh
Crunch, shooo, woosh

Go off the jump, quick icy slide
Trees pass by on either side
Snow in my face, icy and white

Crunch, shooo, woosh
Crunch, shooo, woosh

Joyful and fun
All day on a sled
WHEEEeeeee!

Crunch, shooo, woosh
Crunch, shooo, woosh

—*Jade Johns, age 11, Roxbury*

Awake

Perched anew from the night,
    darkness fades
    to light

Suspended, steady
    rise
    rebirth

Heart hears,
    familiar is
    a robin's song

Could it be true,
    so continually falling
    in love with you

Dear Morning,

—*Juniper Johns, Roxbury*

First Collision

At lacrosse practice, you do what is demanded.
You are told what to do, how to think,
how to be. Run faster. Cover your man.
Stick on stick. Head on a swivel. See
the ball. See your man. But here, now,
your breath drowns out any sideline
insanity, the frothing guidance of coaches.
You're running, faster maybe than
you've ever run, the kind of foot-in-ground
desperation driven only by the pressure
of another. Side by side: you in red and black
and a boy in blue and gold. Sprinting
towards the ball, suddenly you step sideways,
collide, hip and shoulder driven into
hip and shoulder. You feel power move
against power and your power win.
The other boy is gone, fallen away into
the dewy grass. A grey Sunday morning
years ago, and you have learned.

—*Daniel Johnson, Burlington*

I Want to Know Someone Who Calls Me Kitten

after Megan Fernandes

I'm a blizzard of wildflowers and mud.
My raised bed is full of weeds.

I learned from Mother that
there are no amphibians in our lineage
because Hattie Pray froze to death at age 98
while splitting wood and she did not
come back in the spring like the frogs do
in a small parade to their heathen rituals in the vernal
pools.

Some of my rituals might be useful,
but not the ones I obsess over—
those are too heavy,
and you should only hold on to what you can
carry.
The gurus say we are waiting to live instead of living,
but I want to hear,
Keep waiting if you need to, Kitten.

—(Robyn) Joy, Montpelier

Immaculate Reception

In Memory of Franco Harris

Seconds left: the desperate pass
caroms off a defender's chest
toward the ground, as millions gasp
and time expires. Some hold their breath,

waiting a flag that will not come,
some celebrate, but off the screen
a large fullback, his day not done,
scoops the rebound. What might have been

now comes undone, as huge legs plow
across the field for the end zone
and into myth.
                    He is gone now,
with Williams, Russell, Didrikson

and all the rest, human and flawed,
who sparked more joy than any god.

—*Phil Keller, Montpelier*

At Townshend Beach

When I was young, I believed that all grandmothers had
the name Ruby.
 In fields of daisies, summers spun like endless threads of a
golden tapestry.
 I believed I could spread my wings and fly over my house,
my town, and my school.
In dreams of innocence, a heart unburdened, soaring with
untamed glee.

In fields of daisies, summers spun like endless threads of a
golden tapestry.
Beneath the sun's embrace, in barn boots I trod on sands at
Townshend Beach
In dreams of innocence, a heart unburdened, soaring with
untamed glee,
Whispers of safety echoed, a comforting hymn, a lesson to
teach.

Beneath the sun's embrace, in barn boots I trod on sands at
Townshend Beach
Reality brought the truth, awakening my young mind.
Whispers of safety echoed, a comforting hymn, a lesson to
teach,
For even in belief's refuge, shadows of doubt one day would
find.

Beneath the sun's embrace, in barn boots I trod on sands at
    Townshend Beach
Reality brought the truth, awakening my young mind.
For even in belief's refuge, shadows of doubt one day would
    find,
A world not as safe, not as simple, as the dreams once built.

My Grandmother named Ruby was the only thread in life's
    grand quilt,
I learned to trade barn boots for steps on paths yet
    unknown.
A world not as safe, not as simple, as the dreams once built,
But with newfound wisdom, resilience in seeds was sown.

I learned to trade barn boots for steps on paths yet
    unknown,
As summers turned to autumns, and innocence faced the
    tide.
But with newfound wisdom, resilience in seeds was sown,
In the ever-changing rhythm where belief and truth
    coincide.

—*Monda R. Kelley, Brandon*

24 Questions about Love

1. Do you know how much I love you?
2. If love is the answer, can I be more specific?
3. The universe is made of love, nu?
4. How can I love you any more?
5. Does anyone really love me?
6. What is love?
7. Is momentary awareness love?
8. What are the names of everyone you love?
9. Can I go on without your love?
10. You used to love me?
11. What are the Greek names for love?
12. I love what you are doing, thanks?
13. Turn on your love-light baby?
14. Could I "zap" you with love rays?
15. When things work out, don't you just love it?
16. I was scared of being abandoned, why couldn't I trust
    I was loved?
17. What's the opposite of love?
18. What's the power of love?
19. Breathe in love?
20. The active love is sacred?
21. I am loved?
22. How do I love thee?
23. Cover me with your love?
24. If all is love, what next?

—David Klein, Montpelier

Threading the Needle

Slalom skiers intend
to skim gates smoothly.
Bush beating brings
only dead bugs.

When the eye holds truth,
then the little wet thread
wavers to one side
and then the other

before it hits its purpose.
The stickiest wicket
defies straightforward
for little bent lies

recited every day.

—*Tricia Knoll, Williston*

Trimeter After Flood

Because there's beauty too
I take a picture of
a purple bellflower
shaped like a star on
Liberty Street and think
what would Mary Oliver
do? Would she write about
the junk and filth and stink
in the streets, neighborhoods
adjacent to this clean
affluence? Document,
document, witness. When
will this wetness end? Look
here come the scavengers
now in strange cars. I think
every slow moving car
is a trash heap thief. It's
the only time I let
my dog bark & bark & bark.

—*Samantha Kolber, Montpelier*

"Let the way be your seat of honor"

—Rumi

Living the dream pales
to dreaming the dream.
The shiny object
you covet
is tarnished.

The goal always moves away—
the fastest runner in the race.
Success is inferior
to the imagination
so vibrant on the journey.

Force the focus
to the rhythm of your steps
synchronize your breath
to the sparks of your thoughts,
joy is in the Now.

—Kristine Korman, Warren

Walk

Not so long ago
   it was easy
Taken for granted to be done
   with no pain and no real effort
Then age appeared silently,
   stealthily, without respect

When did the spine betray us
   with slippage and compression?
The hip that now aches
   with memories of races easily won

Distance, Time
   Friends once, enemies now
Did we really pedal
   200 miles in a day?
Now we walk
   Grateful for our slow contemplative gait
Thankful to be here this day
   when many are only fading memories
Walking, listening to a cello
   that spoke more than fifty years ago
The artist memorialized
   in binary form as I step 01, 01, 01
Until I am home

—*Ava Lafferty, Lyndonville*

We Must Tend Our Beautiful Earth

Hope is the crocuses
Bursting ephemeral from the snow-frozen ground
Delicate purple blossoms curling open towards the sun
Peace is the loon's call
Mournful song echoing across the lake
Water rippling in the moonlight
Strength is the old oak trees
Firmly rooted in the soil
Green leafy crowns swaying in the breeze
Beauty is the rainwater
Collected in the embrace of a new leaf
Held safely within a flower's cup
Mystery is a cloudless sky
Bright pinpricks of stars
Constellations tracing the heavens
Love is the breeze blowing through the hills
Guiding the bees and butterflies with their nectar
Sending dandelion puffs spinning across the fields
Life is the flowing creek
Dancing through the whorls of ice
Swirls of water ever-moving
Earth is the hands that hold us
The ground that moves beneath our feet
We are the keepers, we must tend to this beautiful world

—*Mayla Landis-Marinello, Middlesex*

Invitation

The world doesn't have to be so beautiful.

The peach doesn't have to be velvet beneath our thumbs
or dripping with goose-bumpy sweetness upon bite.
The furled fern could have been born in a straight shot.
No need to tuck itself
into a downy newborn
before showing us how to rise and open.
And think of the tiny, whimsical forests of moss
that reveal themselves
if you are willing to kneel.
And the pages and pages of the peony,
invitations all,
to bury our noses in summer's elegant fragrance.
And the way snow becomes a quiet blue
if you carve out a hole and peer inside.
And the way my fingers skip across the keyboard this morning
like happy children.

This is not to discount fist and fang,
which, of course, the world is full of.
But remember that the darling blossoms of the apple tree
become nourishing fruit,
delighting us twice for no reason at all.

—M. Latoundji, Walden

Shadows

in mem. my brother Mahlon (1944-1980)

The shade our tamarack throws
Grows paler every day,
Just as its needles do.
Each last needle will soon have fallen.
An evergreen, in short, that's not.
How can you be more than forty years dead?
I look up from writing this,
and it's painful, my perception,
as though I had some something
in my eyes, almost
like a needle itself.

Those eyes, against my will, go blurry.
Again. The rain's a subtle drum
on every tree in the forest,
but I focus on the one.
I've gotten so used to it.
It's stood apart for most of my life.
Four decades and more without you now.
That single tree is spilling itself
on the ground but in mind, the dark shadow
of its canopy will live on

even after it's gone.

—*Sydney Lea, Newbury*

The Old

Our backs
Are now bent
Our eyes
Could see better
Our legs
Move with effort
Our arms
Can't carry much.

We once were
The New:
Builders of Bridges
Makers of Roadways
Keepers of Forests.

We now are
The Old:
Sharers of Stories
Town Criers of Truth
Sages of Villages.

We are
The Old.

We are here.

—*Maxine Leary, Montpelier*

Boreal (Entropy)

petals
hopeful
for dawn
crave rotted oakflesh
flake and fall
into the
calling
waiting
worm mouths
tiny trillium stems
moss barnacles
tangled
root tendrils
soak up
fevered soil
to grow ferns
and float new spores.

Every pattern alive
Leans in the same way:
To trick food,
to sip at light.

—*Maggie Lenz, Montpelier*

1-10 (and Back Again)

Poetry
They say
Is just words
How hard is that?
When you put them together
What are you trying to convey
That won't be clearer posed in prose?

Ah, poetry you reply, layers beauty and form
Constraints not faced when rules allow you endless paragraphs.
Poetry thrives inside the fenceposts of precision, timing, and rhythm
While prose frolics amidst the wildflowers of open meadows.
They are both honorable paths pursuing their goals
To broaden readers' horizons and spark imagination

Above all, tell a good story.
It's not really about labels
Or fitting the box
Except for poems
Like this
One

—*Michael Levine, Middlesex*

PoemCity

it's difficult to write,
this thought
these scribblings
that try to speak
to others.
and to fashion them all
into a predetermined form—
twenty-four lines,
no more—
it's a struggle to say
anything at all worth saying.
here, halfway there,
leaning on a lamppost
waiting for a train
catching a bus
looking for someone
through this window
who might pause to
look into these words
to divine meaning
to see beyond
and come out
the other side
intact

—*craig line, Calais*

Casting Seeds

Turn your face to catkins, violet flowers,
and crows pecking black soil.
Witness the mystery of what will be given,
of what you might write down
after grass dies back.
What happens between the black
that comes before and after light
is an unfolding of days,
a collection of letters
sent from the moments that changed you,
stamped by seasons, and read again
and again as memories,
the soul's shaping in this bundle
of yellowed papers tied with kitchen twine.

—Lisa, East Montpelier

Love Poem to a Library

How can I say
which book I love the most—
it's like asking
which is my favorite child—
easier to say I love the library.
As I walk up granite steps
out of rain and sleet
through the portico
into the reading room,
paper hearts made of poems
hang everywhere.
I wander to fiction stacks,
but stop at Calder's "Animals,"
lithographic red and yellow cats
scampering with an elephant,
and glance up at a Grecian frieze.
I head for art books,
move on to the history shelves,
then get distracted
by poetry posters everywhere.
Oh library,
the more I check you out,
the more I realize it's you I love.

—*George Longenecker, Middlesex*

About Grief

its a grief not rooted in need,

but in dreams.

a grief that floats away

as i look out across the water,

see trees holding hands,

reflection of sky kissing the surface blue,

feeling one, but separate from sadness.

somewhere along the days of my life, maybe in the crib,

i learned to allow grief its freedom

to roll out like waves

accept and yield to it washing over me like an ocean,

building up, letting go, below, over and under, like tides.

it's not held in my body.

it has a power of its own that makes things move.

it dwells in a seaweed forest, with sea creatures

and schools of colors that swim around and through the
     coral reefs.

yet, i can find it just below the surface of stillness,

when there are no ripples or winds at the shore,

as i remember, ponder, cry, do what it is i do.

—*Jesse LoVasco, East Montpelier*

Nothing You Need

Pass this poem by, neighbor.
It has no sordid similes, no skipping rhymes.
No lingering regrets. Nobody sings.

There are no sly, scriptural allusions,
no deep dive into metaphor;
nobody high dives into a small tub of bliss.

It might once have had simpering flutes
or an oboe tuning up an orchestra in Bern.
It seems the boyish trombones, blaring trumpets,
even the savvy saxophones have gone.

No wild nights with neon, no screeching tires.
No kitchen knives. No rivulets of blood or tears.
No unreliable narrator who would have you
believe him handsome. No lies.

Come to think of it, no pithy sayings
and no jokes.

A daydream of lost love, maybe?
A foundling in swaddling clothes?
Alas. Nothing you can take away.

Unless what you really wanted
was this glimpse of your own, comely face
in the storefront window glass.

—*Daniel Lusk, Burlington*

Family

Found poem: source text: "With Housing Tight New Vermont Teachers Crash at an Inn," Anne Wallace Allen, Seven Days, September 5, 2022.

All
Stay around
Town
We're not victims
Trying to help
Many love the light
And
Beauty.

—River M., Cabot

Reflected Light

I am reading about
John Singer Sargent's
Luminous understanding of
Reflected light or "light bounce,"
The term, painter, Robert Wade uses.
And, in Wade's study of Sargent,
He writes, with excitement,
How reflected light has reflected color,
How shadows are far from gray.
I have become "observer"
An old painter learning
New ways to see.

—*Sandra Maccarrone, Montpelier*

Almanac

It was in the dead air
Between the end of the call about contracts
And the beginning of the call about budgets
That I saw it,
At the center of a perfect snapshot
Of a mushy mid-March morning,
When fifty degrees, a crispy sky, and scudding clouds
Made the inside window frames damp.
There it was, hovering near the glass outside.
It was a solitary fly,
A glorious black jewel
Buzzing against the eggshell-colored spaces
Between the house and the forest,
Signaling the triumph of hope over experience.
I wondered if it knew the forecast
And whether it would seek the shelter
Of my eaves in the squall arriving after teatime.
Maybe it knew the weather and didn't care,
Being told by a better almanac than mine
Of the coming of the kingdom of the Sun.

—*Michael Madill, West Topsham*
previously published online at michaelmadill.medium.com

Mortal Down

In heaven's crying room,
which is deep blue like the ocean,
and is scented with parma violets
and jasmine;
where angels cry
and the lady made of moon-foam
sits between Artemis and Athena.
They gaze upon the mortal woman
below,
lovingly, sadly.
She goes down into the river
in desperation,
beneath the moon.
Have pity on this mortal woman.
She is drowning from pain and love.
And the wind roars.

—*Kimberly Madura, Essex*

Leaving Iowa City / The Right Questions

When you asked me
to take photos of my trip,
I knew you meant
just a few
to share when I got back home.

On the second evening I remembered
my promise. I had spent the day lost
in the blur of my country
just beyond the bus window:

the bored reflection of a little girl
in the row ahead of mine
was cast across sunset plains
while her mother spoke in hushed tones
about being brave.

       A camera can hold all that light in place
       if we know what to ask of it.

But my fingers have been fumbling
at the controls and I can't seem to find

the right questions.

—*Jack Markoski, Montpelier*

Take Blue

River stones pale as ice,
summer sky simmering with July heat,
mountains on the horizon a ridge of ocean waves,
azure seas curved around the contours of earth,
cobalt fins darting, a ribbon winding down a young girl's braid,
eager sailors in royal navy suits pressing the prow toward port.

Take blue: winging wide as buntings or jays,
great herons in flight, a nest full of robin's eggs,
long-armed delphinium, cornflower,
the splendid bonnets of Texas,
denim stained by berries,
a bruise swelling, water pooling,
cooling distant stars,
my father's eye.

Take blue, this one thing you think you know,
Take it now and knead it in your palms like bread,
pour it into your hands like paint, like rain,
sapphire wings brushing your brow
blood pulsing beneath skin,
brimming indigo night beneath which
the wild and brilliant iris blooms.

—*Katherine H. Maynard, South Burlington*

The Legacy of Elms

What I remember from childhood
was not so much their stateliness––their
hallelujahs of upward limbs poising
in procession up the long avenues––

but the day they came down: how the tall
plumb ranks they formed suddenly tumbled
into jumbles of sticks and stumps, and the for-
granted shade they gave left forever,

so even the cloudiness of that day
had the blinding effect of making
the world too bright to really see.

Decades later, I found one last tree, alone,
in a field, its limbs lifting the air back up
as if loss had no weight, no substance at all.

—*Tim Mayo, Brattleboro*
previously published in *Rat's Ass Review*, Summer 2019

Tree of Solitude

"In the midst of the crowd keep with perfect sweetness the independence of solitude…"
  —Ralph Waldo Emerson, "Self-Reliance"

tis an awakening to see oneself
among the many trees in the forest

standing in the shadows of greatness
on a midsummer morning

when sunlight streaks past
with its sharp edged rays

like a blade of shining glory
cutting through the falsity

of the forest for the trees

—Elizabeth McCarthy, Walden
from *Wild Silence*, forthcoming from Kelsay Books

In your next letter

Please tell me if you still walk
through the beautiful cemetery
where we walked once so long ago,
and do you go alone, think about
those buried there,

do you wonder
about their names, how long they lived,
what made their hearts beat faster, whether
they slept too long, or not enough
before falling into final sleep.

Tell me do their souls walk with you
consoling you with their quietude,
soothing your jangled worries
as you wait for Christmas to be over,
the house clean again, put back to rights?

Please tell me if someone has shoveled
a walkway for you to meander through
the headstones and breathe in the cold December air.

And—*especially*—please tell me
what color is your hat as you walk
through this sacred ground,
how it feels on your head,
and if it is warm enough.

—*Florence McCloud, South Burlington*

Mother-In-Law in the Bardo

Was it because we took the bracelet,
your bracelet, studded with diamonds,
sapphires and other precious stones,
the one you gave our daughter—
who, by the way, would never wear it—
to sell at auction? Or perhaps it was
the Louis XV style loveseat, upholstered
in floral chintz, standing on cabriole legs,
too low to sit in comfortably,
too fussy for our house? Yes,
it's true, I've listed it on Facebook
Marketplace though we've had no bites.
So why put on such a show?
To fling yourself, in the middle of the night,
from wall to stairs to the front hall floor?
I admit, it was spooky. The photo of
you looking up the stairs at me, not a crack
in the glass, not a fissure in the frame,
just a bit of severed twine. Don't whine.
Give it up, move on, it's been fifteen years
for God's sake. You can't take it with you.

—*Hatsy McGraw, Hartland*

Winter, Vermont

I.
The dog, in her first
Vermont winter: bounding
through thigh-high
snowdrifts,
equal parts   joy
      and desperation
on her face.
The wonder of it, and the
suffocating

               terror
of the unknown.

II.
What is left
when the mind clears?
The snowdrift
(caught)
between two buildings;
less a pile than
a soft settling. The unintentional
inescapable
eiderdown of thought
waiting for the thaw.

—*Kelly McMahon, Montpelier*

In the Nest of Night

The Milky Way astonishes him.
He marvels at the banner of light
overhead. A murmuration of stars.

He wants to see it once more
before their return home, but
on this night the gibbous moon

takes center stage and obscures stars
in its yellow light. On any other night
we would welcome a moon

bright enough to illumine a path
through a tangle of trees. Wonder
enlarges and diminishes us.

Behind the moon, the black nest of night
brims with stars fledged aeons ago.
I imagine the stilling of wings

as myriad stars settle, save one
that swoops through velvet darkness.

—*Rebecca McMeekin, Braintree*

At My Sister's

It's another sunny day,
two projects planned—
weeding the back flower bed,
and repairing Mother's falling-apart quilts.
Her fingers didn't work too good
those last few years,
but she kept cranking them out.
We all have several—I ended up with five,
and could have had more,
but ran out of places to put them
in my pint-size apartment.
They got smaller and smaller
as she neared 100 years old,
and you had to watch out for straight pins
she missed when she finished them up.
Busy, busy, busy, she always
had to be doing something, if not the quilts
then those nylon scrubbies for washing dishes.
I hoarded those, knowing at some point
there'd be an end to them.
And there was,
there was.

—Joanne Mellin, Winooski

Silver Maple Story

Gnarled, knotty charcoal claws, concrete clutching.
Hard crust tangles above
Soft veiny strings below fading and gasping—
struggling to feed, nourish.

Decline quiet and slow ... still body stands,
shining a sky-touch fading green with bareness peeking.
How long before hidden systems sleep?
How long until the end manifests?

Rot. Tumble. Enrichment of earth.
Swirl of the silver seed.
Precious process.
Full, empty, filling.

—*Christine Corrigan Mendez, Burlington*

Luna Moth

On silken wing, an alien queen
flew soft upon the breeze,
and landed on my window screen—
to rest there, at her ease.

I watched her feathered headgear wave;
her hindwings curved below.
The streaming silver moonlight gave
her form a ghostly glow.

Her downy body, mouthless face,
and dewy, lime-green wing
lent Luna moth an eerie grace,
mysterious as Spring.

—*Christy Mihaly, East Calais*

previously published in the anthology *The Bee is not Afraid of Me: A Book of Insect Poems*, The Emma Press

Shoe Laces

I keep tying and untying my shoelaces
splitting hairs over definitions
in the absence of meanings
like little dolls bundled preterm
on the hospital floor
cold like the memories of tortured pasts
genocide, holocausts
8 million then now unimaginable
to the point of forgetting
where we came from
why we are here

—*Steve Minkin, Brattleboro*

Broken

This world has no mercy
for the things it has broken. Like
that yearling with its two
front legs snapped, remember? How
she kept trying to raise herself
to her full height, her bullion fur,
its wisps of white, caked
in mud, each time she drove herself,
plunging back into the earth. And perhaps
I am right to gather the covers
tightly around myself, to polish my armor, scour
and buff it into a golden
shine, so all you can see is your own reflection. We
are grateful to see ourselves,
reflected, the illusion we
are safe, but still
I remember that yearling, bleating
in the forest, the sound of it, I
lay my palm on her torso, her shallow breath
and tiny heartbeat, held her
to this fragile earth. Eyelids falling
in one long out breath, she
craned up her neck, lifting her face
to the vast cathedral of the birch trees,
emerald leaves illuminated
by the sun, falling in the west.

—Benjamin L. Mitchell, *Westminster*

Reverberation

Marconi thought no sound was ever lost
but echoed fainter and finer
in every other sound.

I know how the words of the day
return by night in the small talk
of the chimney and the eaves
between two and four.

All night the trees
were walking in the wind.
At any time the murmuring
of mice might reassemble
in the great-horned owl's
scream.

—*Richard W. Moore, Burlington*

For Poetry

For my teacher's teachers

The poem is a woman bathed in light
Who hears the strain of things dying to be heard.

Bonds of love cut like Castilian roses
On the tissue thin skin of the back of your hand.

For her, yellow corn on a white platter
Is an illumination served by unseen hands.

Darkness is not a metaphor — cloud cover
And obsidian are the purposeful shapes of tears.

For her, the universe is not concealed
Nor sweeps in from afar. It's sensed at first electrically,

A ghostly hum that quails the poet's pen—
And brings the starved to her door.

—Karen Morris, Barre

The Stag

Hunting season survived,
antlers intact from bucks' attacks
and not yet shed, the stag bends
to drink where the spring flows
into the pond. Wait. Nose up, ears
like radar, he spots the artist, watches
her inch her Canon to her eye.

Not from fear but from joy
he bounds off, slips
through white pines
into the forest.

She shot his image a millisecond before,
then painted him until her vision, his
likeness, lights up the gallery, the hospice
hallway, or your living room wall. He's
a fellow creature with no desire
for pretenses or disguises. He can
be trusted in his beauty
and his readiness.

—*Nicola Morris, Plainfield*

November

The gaudy time is over.
Now is the time of tarnished gold,
burnt sienna, and rusty brown.
We clear dried stalks from the garden,
gather seed heads and chestnuts.
Now we say farewell with no assurance
that winter will be kind.
We turn away from the woods
and the hungry deer.
We close the curtains
and take refuge in cider and pie.
We curl under the comforter
with the purring cat
and the books we had no time for in summer
and let life narrow.
We great each dawn
as a promise
that things will change and change
and spring will come again.

—B. Morrison, Brattleboro

Deer on the move: Road Sign on I 91, November

Against the blaze of golden-
rod yellow and blood-red maple
the deer cross
alert for food
or shelter or a mate.

I have never hit a deer
but once, on a darker,
different road a moose flashed
past, catching the front fender
and headlight of my car

at night. So fast, I was sure
we had both escaped
damage. It's true, what they say:
all you see are legs, nothing
that signals animal.

More like tall sticks
or upright tent stakes. Gone
before the mind registers
pain or collision.

Don't leave, deer.
Don't leave, leaves.
Wait, winter, so little
light ahead of us.

—*Barbara E. Murphy, Burlington*

life for life

it stirs
pale infant force
coalescing around kernel
breaching surface
thin fingers of being
open to the radiant sun
and she is clothed in purpose
breathing in waste laden airs
before exhalations of oxygen
transmuting light into sweetness
sugared sustenance for her children
she is alive to spangled skies
she is rooted in dark soils
for a time...
and in senescence
the mysterious flame
moves on
the exchange
of life
for life

—*elizabeth murmuring, Barre*
previously published online at allpoetry.com/elizabeth_murmuring

A Snow Squall Arrives

I stopped at my window so I could look out and see the
 different layers
Of hills going into the distance, as well as groups of
 evergreens that
Were also layered and closer to me than the hills, a few of
 them were
Scattered and very close. When I returned a few minutes
 later I couldn't
Believe my eyes as I saw a snow squall moving toward me
 over the hills
And beginning to erase everything it passed in a
 combination of blowing
Snow flakes, gray fog, and clouds, finally reaching me and
 my house when
All I could see were snow flakes wrapped in gray. Then I
 watched as the
Squall disappeared and returned a couple of times, moving
 in and out of
The world around me until after the final exit, when I saw a
 spectacular
Presentation of bright sunlight on the horizon, mixing with
 the light and dark
Fluffy clouds and a touch of pale blue sky. After a while
 somehow everything
I had been looking at was slowly transforming into a sunset
 of many
Different pinkish colors accented by a variety of dark
 dancing cloud shapes

—*Joan Murray, Worcester*

long distance

late nights feel like a hammer inside my skull
eyes burning, staring through the screen for hours
searching desperately for the memory of what we used to be
sitting on your bedroom floor, laughing the same air

eyes burning, staring through the screen for hours
lesser, though, to the pain splitting open my chest
sitting on your bedroom floor, laughing the same air
a feeling of warmth since unmatched

lesser, though, to the pain splitting open my chest
it's been months, but the wound still bleeds
a feeling of warmth since unmatched
as my fingers trail through the blood, still searching,
    searching

it's been months, but the wound still bleeds
searching desperately for the memory of what we used to be
as my fingers trail through the blood, still searching,
    searching
i miss you.

—*Beck Natale, Colchester*

The Summer of Smoke

Wildfires consume the north, closing in.
Haze obscures the mountain view from our home,
a former weekend ski cabin for flatlanders. Now ours.

Haze obscures my thoughts, too, shifting and impossible to grasp,
like smoke. It's been more than two months and the pain
    has not abated,
perhaps dulled a bit, like an old kitchen knife, still full of hurt.

I mourn something that never was, a life I did not have, a life
    that will never be.
It's impossible to see clearly, impossible to imagine it will
    ever change.
The haze will be here all summer, they say. Perhaps longer
    for me.

Water does not bring relief, nor do the things people say.
    Normal. Common.
At least.

Fires rage, inside and out. Tears come easily now.

How do we clear the fog, see through the smoke?
    How will I heal?
How long will this go on?

—*Erika Nichols-Frazer, Waitsfield*

Even the dreams of James Joyce

Even the dreams
of James Joyce
The biggest poet of our time
Are gone:
Triest at night is desolated,
Like if nobody ever lived there.
No lights.
The Dead.
Wind howling up our shaky
Stairs like there was never been
A city there.
With his astute pointy beard,
His English lessons at the Berlitz School...
He's gone.
And we lived our Bohemia
In this forgotten place
Which only the memory
Can revisit.

—*Nitya, Barre*

A Perfect Day

Harold and Button walked downtown to have a bite to eat.
Harold had a pizza pie and Button got to sleep.

Harold and Button go to the park to run and stretch their feet.
Harold throws a Frisbee disk and Button gets to leap.

Harold and Button head back home as the sun begins to set.
Harold puts his feet up and Button gets to rest.

Harold and Button went to bed at the end of a perfect day.
Harold dreamed of lollipops and Button dreamed of play.

—*Penny Nolte, Montpelier*

ocean grove

it's heavy
with heaviness added
notarize the sky
send it away to the earth
the trees know when it rains
'cause the roots are connected to the sky
in ocean grove
'cause the trees are connected to the sky
and the trees know when it rains
'cause the roots are connected to the sky
in ocean grove
it's heavy
with heaviness added

—*Travis Alden Nutting, Middlesex*

Ten-Day Silent Retreat

All my brothers shuffle
as if, off to the gallows or they just got off a hard day's ride.

Hold onto something strong,
lash yourself to that rock. The masks of Mara
are many and you vowed to reveal them all.

The rings of an oak tree and my fingerprints are similar.
Could we be related?

They say just before an earthquake
or a great fire all the animals in the forest flee.

This morning, there!
Behind the pagoda
on her side, lies an oak grandmother.

Her scabby trunk,
a condo complex
for red squirrels.
Mosses sprout, slugs frolic, mushrooms rejoice.

If not for her son's trunk she would surely yield
to gravity and roll into the stream bed.

—Kevin O'Keefe, *West Brattleboro*

Bilingual (Japanese/English) Tankas

洪水のわが町の4時目覚むればいつもと違う鳥のコーラス
Kouzuino wagamachinoyoji mezamureba itsumotochigau
    torinokoorasu
waking up at 4am
my beloved town
is flooded
birds singing
a different tune

道は川パトカーは船オール漕ぎひとつひとつの窓を確かむ
Michiwakawa patokaawafune oorukogi hitotsuhitotsuno
    madootashikamu
street is a river
police car is a boat
patrolling with oars
checking windows
one by one

天が泣き川の怒りが溢れ出し涙満ちゆくわが街の道
Tenganaki kawanoikariga afuredashi namidamichiyuku
    wagamachinomichi
the sky is crying
the anger of the river
is overflowing
the streets of my town
filled with tears

—*Michiko Oishi, Montpelier*
  (English translations with Rhea Costantino)

Grandpa

At the Dark of Moon
with hands like old roots
he cradles lineal bulbs,
seeds of his father and his,
talks to them in thick words
that enlarge the task.

He stands bent to a trust,
thunder punctuates his purls;
I step back,
he senses alarm,
takes my hand;
We walk before rain.

On a rise facing south we pause;
He sets his children softly down,
digs each grave
six inches to a tee,
lays history to rest
for another season.

The earth holds no raven
he says in benediction
The earth is true

—*Richard Fischer Olson, Montpelier*

Something to that Effect

Just so you know,
there is no excuse for driving like that,
even as you're dodging potholes
yet it might be true
that you haven't had a few,
but then sometimes all it takes
is a slow metabolism or low blood sugar
although it's good to keep in mind therefore that,
because of this, and until otherwise pointed out,
and agreed upon, the thing to remember is
either the aforementioned fact
or else to sign the dotted line
rather than walking it.

—Ann Onymous, Moscow

To my slow toddler

Had we but world enough and time
you'd push all the buttons and visit every floor from 1 to 24.
You'd take three hours to eat your Cheerios
and spend whole afternoons zipping and unzipping your jacket.
We'd read *Cars and Trucks and Things That Go* a hundred
    times a day
and listen to your favorite 10-second loop
of *3, 2, 1... Blastoff* until all the stars faded from the sky

Always I hear about time's winged chariot:
how fast you'll grow, how little I'll catch.
Maybe I should be more sentimental.

But no, right now, we are late
friends are waiting
I am hungry
and tired
and I dream at night of cars and trucks
and also of things that go
of which you are not one
because you are
so slow.

—*Holly Painter, South Burlington*
previously published in *Meow Meow Pow Pow*, April 2019

Jane Doe

dead night headlights,
woman—
forest burning

blades of grass reaching
in moonlight

antler locked in spell—
divine intent.

woman—nameless
migration
across landscape

to find
water

that isn't her ancestry.

trees wide open,
bushes crouched in labor

june beetles
call her name out
like a siren

fishtail necklace hung with
a broken teacup frame of
starshine

smoky eye, smoky clouds
hiding bruises that mark land
    like
it's a plan
for where to lay the next
bomb

—*Emma Paris, Putney*

Free Pile

I put the last of
the baby stuff out
by the road with
a sign that said "free." which
is how most of it came
to us: the tub we propped up
'cause it was missing a leg,
the sled with its second
replacement rope, the
twenty-one alphabet blocks,
the push truck I'm grateful
never made a sound—
all of it was gone within
the hour. Scooped up
by someone who needs
what we no longer
need—
saved from
the slow demise of
being kept, unused,
"in case"

—*Devon Parish, Montpelier*

Beluga

for Lucille

On the ochre March lawn
a length of blue plastic baling twine
beside it a black two-inch
piece of flexible garden hose.

They were the mouth and eye
of the beluga whale we summoned
from that last heavy gift of snow
a month ago. Blue line

as mouth dark plastic eye
brought the snow to life,
as though the spirit of a whale
might pay a two-week visit. It was

a hurried sculpture   improbably
short   tail raised unbelievably
high   and yet our yard assumed
the welcome of an arctic bay.

I watch the chickadee beside
the redpoll at our feeder—one
with a map for staying, the other
leaves tomorrow for the tundra.

And my favorite aunt slipped
off with ease and gratitude
as her husband gently said,
to some other jurisdiction.

—*Scudder H. Parker, Middlesex*

Homesteading in Vermont

After the fortieth death of evening grey
you know that winter finally has you.
You read dead authors and wait for May.
Dark inviting water freezes white capped blue.
When a goose's webbed feet fuse with ice,
you know that winter finally has you.
Nothing to do but cook some rice,
no point in letting the coyotes eat well,
when a goose's webbed feet fuse with ice.
Her wings fluttered when your axe fell.
You accept the goose and her bad luck.
No point in letting the coyotes eat well.
In the dark you gut her and pluck.
Feathers become fistfuls of flowers for her wake.
You accept the goose and her bad luck.

I think you foresaw, and enjoy, winter's blood-dark ache.
After the fortieth death of evening grey,
feathers become fistfuls of flowers for her wake.
You read dead authors and wait for May.

—Rolf Parker-Houghton, Brattleboro
forthcoming in the *Lyric*

On The La Platte

Turtles, motionless as Zen masters,
pose on every sunlit log, practicing
the art of synchronized sitting.

A Caspian Tern, hunched in mid-air,
hovers for a moment before becoming
a missile aimed inexorably at its target.

The Great Blue Heron stands like a stone
in the shallows, teaching us the gift
of patience and of knowing when to strike.

The river, slow and unassuming, holds us
all aloft, the fish and feathered ones,
this human, breathless in her handmade boat.

—*Angela Patten, Burlington*

January

Snow curls off the roof
like a white wave

We shovel until our backs hurt

The cold like a hard slap
on our cheeks

The sheep
dressed in wool
look at us through their fence
Smug

February
arrives without fanfare
light returns

Pots of tiny crocus shoots on our kitchen counter
Garden for now.

—*Melissa Perley, Berlin*

Spelling the News

After the rage in barrage & tragedy;
The scar in miscarry & scarcity;
The stolen rib in retribution;
After the late cut across circumlocution;
The reach and ache in treachery;
The triumphal arch of patriarchy;
After the pit in spite & capitalism;
The silent oath below loathing;
The hate embedded in whatever;

Remember our stance: resistance—
to nest in greenest amnesty.
As we age in any language,
hear the heart. The use of a pause
is the hum in humus, even posthumous.
Here, unwithered,
may plea & sure still join for pleasure.
Let love spillover.

—Verandah Porche, Guilford

Heartbeat

She flips and flops and twirls,
    tosses one pillow, grabs another,
grabs a blanket, throws it from the bed.
    Shhh, I say, but she just mumbles, *I can't sleep.*
      She says, *Look at my eyes.* They are open.
Goodnight, I say, and before she can move, I set my head on her
    chest.
    Little Girl is a flutter of hummingbirds beating.
      A banging bass drum, cadencing fast.
I keep my head there, listening, hearing her heart.
    It sings, *No sleep, no sleep, no sleep*
      until slowly the humming settles beneath my ear,
until slowly Little Girl quiets beneath the weight of my
    head,
    the weight of her fatigue.
      Her body calming, heartbeat slowing.
Now, exactly in beat with her inhalations, exhalations.
    Slowly, gently, heart-beating her way into sleep.

—Sean Prentiss, Woodbury
previously published in Talking River Review, January 2024

Long Love

blur of years stirs in the room
on a bright February morning

I have studied your face
for ten thousand days

long shadows across the untouched snow
your winter-split fingertips against my spine

tone color of your voice
that has said my name more than any other

ragged with grief, hoarse with desire
warm tenor of dailiness

when our love was illegal
and we were young we promised

not to promise, didn't we
didn't we say we would just begin again

—Alison Prine, Burlington

previously published in the anthology *The Wonder of Small Things, Poems of Peace and Renewal*, Storey

Love at first sight

Boarded on a plane,
With so many thoughts in my brain
My 1 year old on lap,
She was so in a mood for a nap
I googled the distance,
It showed 8000 miles of en-dur-ance
Luggages, port of entry, after all that gap,
Finally settled in a six seater cab
Gazing out the window,
I raised my eyebrow
My heart was racing,
As she looked astonishing
All my pain was worthier,
I am so in love with you, Montpelier!

—*Parvathi Rajaram, Montpelier*

Worksong

A swung hammer strikes the head of the nail.
The scythe undercuts the sun shaft of wheat.
Milk wrung from udder into waiting pail.
The loom shudders to its blended fabric beat.

Bricks tucked in beds of mortar, each on each.
Shingles arranged like chainmail to the skies.
Steel beams fastened across the river's breach.
A letterpress quoin filled with leaden lies.

I admire work that leaves something behind,
that builds, and makes, and creates to an end,
over commodity trades, contracts signed.
From farmers with calloused palms, I descend.

My own work by hand and sweat, tile and blade,
lumber of forests lost put to good use,
more honest inch by inch, flaws tailor-made.
Even hangmen take care to tie the noose.

When I wake to another spin on earth
let me burn my day with labor's rich worth
and leave the toil of the abstracted kind
in the offices of the absent mind.

—*Kiev Rattee, Manchester*

Afternoon at Sea

I am ten years old,
tired and barefoot,
floating on the unsteady sea of a kitchen floor I rarely stand on.
My only father leans against a white stove eating curried rice.
He makes a mess, spilling rice on the hard blue tile,
blurring the sea a dull shade of blood.
He tells me to clean it up
and I obey.
Because I am his first-born child.
Because when I am with him, I forget how to swim.

—Deidra K. Razzaque, Brattleboro

At The Last

Those leaves, the last gold ones
surely do not hang on for hope.
They have watched their neighbors fall,
felt the loosening of their own stems,
devoid of green.
They know the inevitability of wind.

They are more like
the band on the Titanic
as they played "Nearer My God To Thee"
taking courage from a last blaze
of music or gold

Giving the rest of us
a small sliver of light
before the icy dark.

I am humbled
by such brave generosity
At the last.

—*Susan Reid, Montpelier*

The spray of lilies

is at the end of its run.
One blossom has already been clipped
and composted
Two remain.

One drops its petals
brown at the tips
limp, beyond the days of pollinator fascination.

Tilting toward the remaining flower,
which throws perfect petals wide,
thrusting pistils toward the ceiling.

Blooming and beyond
spending recklessly, and spent,
they fill the air with scent
as if to say with remaining breath

"Life is short, who knows, even fruitless.
But how will we know
unless we give it all we've got!?"

—*Susan Reid, Montpelier*

Love Is

A word, a feeling, an expression, flowers, candy
Off key singing, enchanting, a baby's first smile
Simple, complex, tears, laughs, expansive, four letters
a puppies sweet face, a joyous merry go round.

Love listens, likes, lingers, lacks logic, lures, lyric
Love is lovely, loyal, longevity.
Love makes one loveable, loony, lucky
Love is laughter, life, lively
Love makes one lilting, likeable
Love is lust, luxuriant, life long.

Love makes one lithe, leap, limitless
Love is loving, lifting luscious
Love makes one luminous, limber, light
Love is luster, limelight, lilacs.

Love is for me, for you, for us, for the world
For the environment, for peace, for life
For the universe, for young and old.

Love is LOVE is love.

—*Vera Resnik, Warren*
previously published in *Jo Lee Magazine*, 2018

Aquamarine

Aquamarine, aquamarine
Don't think that I've forgotten you!
I well recall those days of green,
Altho they were in all too few.

Aquamarine, aquamarine
Why did I ever let you go?
Might have been fear that came between
Just know that I regret it so.

Aquamarine, aquamarine
Please know that I do think of you!
Were we still in those days of green,
I'd hold you close, aquamarine.

—Michael Roach, Montpelier

December Blues

And yet again Chrissy won't be the same this year
You'll be ten thousand miles and an ocean away
 sitting in the pool with prawns and beer
The sky that unique hue of Aussie Blue
I'll be next to the fire with glög in hand, literally living a
     different day, wishing I was
back home

You'll drag out the willow and play before the sun gets too
     high;
nick behind, over the fence, six-and-out
While we sit inside and watch Ralphy take his eye out again
     with that Red Rider
(you know, the one with the compass in the stock)
You're in the sun and I'm in the snow, I'd do anything to
     escape and just go, go,
go...

Your glasses will clink over Christmas dinner as the sun
     drops through a sultry
evening sky; chilled wine and pink cheeks, tinged from a
     day of delight in the
warm sun
Whilst my eight year old will wake me with excited cries
     about Santa
Breakfast, lunch, full roast with fixin's, drinks with the in-laws,
All in the bitter cold, despite a bright red sun

—Greg Robertson, Northfield

Nature

I hear rain drops
I hear singing birds
I hear dogs barking
I hear myself thinking

I see snow that fell out of the sky and trees
The snowflakes are falling down on the ground

I am dirt; I am one with the earth
A rock is different from dirt but I do not care
that it is different;
I am who I am

—Margo Robertson, age 9, Northfield

Then Dust

From glaciers far, mountains near
rivers recent to this shore
the rock in my hand
a softly rounded, flat
quartz white stone with smooth
orange edges in my grip
whips with my hurling arm
skipping, sidetracked in its
journey to becoming sand.

—Bruce Jefferson Rose, Monkton
previously published online at allpoetry.com, January 2024

Evening from a Window

I wait with the world for soon-coming eve
for the quieting when workday's zeal abstains
for the time when the brightness of doing takes leave
and the cool shade of resting comes o'er me again

slowly a settling settles on all
the world in colors of wheat now reclines
the sky fills with gold as shadows grow tall
the wood of my room and as deepens and shines

deep skies urge us leave today's shortfalls behind
the clouds, longing-full, all our sins to forgive
a sigh fills the air, the sun's drooping eyes find
day's bustle to die, a glad stillness to live

but darker grows darker and coolness grows cold
the world a stranger in angles of night
till soft upon blankets mind's gnarls unfold
till dreaming at last all eye's burdens makes light

—*Andrew Ross, Montpelier*

A good death

If you are very blessed,
death will visit you
on quiet feet.

If you are thus blessed,
death shows you their face
lined with a past of smiles.

You are held
a grip firm, but
oh, so soft

I see you drift away.

You and Death hold
each other aloft.

Oh, how I wish
you could stay
or I could come

But Death tells
me softly, let
go. And I do.

—Jenny Rossi, Winooski

Reflecting on Robert Bly's *Silence in the Snowy Fields*

I've read this book at least ten times
or maybe twenty
and I don't always get what he says
but his easy saying
is always a comfort.
His poems about wide open Midwest
winter fields get me every time.

Lose ambition and see
with clear eyes he says,
approximately.
Choose your own angle of ascent.
I get it.

I too have wasted time
driving around
in a world bright
with reflected moonlight,
sounds of the village
muffled by snow pack.

—*Charles Rossiter, Bennington*
a different version of this poem was published in *Verse-Virtual,* January 2024

Returning Home

found poem: source text: The Perks of Being a Wallflower, *Stephen Chbosky*

One o'clock in the morning.
Terrible returning home.
Didn't feel right.
Just sat in the front door.
Which made me feel so bad.
I cry.
Better start being honest
about how I feel.

—*Aysha Mae Russell, Marshfield*

Beach Dancing

She went to the lighthouse to dance by the sunset,
I went to write a poem.
Her bare feet leave dents and bumps in the sand,
Her shoulders sway to the music in her mind.
Dancing as if no one was watching,
no one except her mother—notebook on my knees,
scribbling poems about crows, raindrops, the moon.
My eyes can't help but look up—
Does either know how beautiful they are?
The sunset—
its deep orange trail shimmering to the foamy edges.
And my teenage daughter—
soaking in each moment of our Ogunquit getaway.
The sun disappears behind her,
too soon, too soon,
and time to return to our room.

—*Martha Anderson Sanborn, Vergennes*

Aging

I can wait in line at the supermarket,
Judging the man, who, like myself, is slow:
Slow to find his credit card,
Slow to pack his groceries.
Or I can know that we are the same, he and I,
Living through this phase of our lives:
Sad to be so slow,
Embarrassed to be keeping people waiting.

Or perhaps not.
Perhaps only accepting our place in this life,
Shuffling along,
Perhaps to Buffalo,
Or perhaps to the exit doors,
To the bright sun and cool breeze and unexpected peony
    outside.
Remembering this sensation,
The smell of crisp late spring,
Feeling it in every cell,
With joy.
Or perhaps with a sudden pang of fear
Because I can't be here with energy to burn,
As in the past.
Because I will never again hike
To the summit of Mount Abraham.

—*Sam Sanders, Montpelier*

Invisible Matters

Does time exist outside itself
or does time exist inside curious circles
we are wound tight around?
In some cases, daylight leaves no trace
in the space between dusk's shadow.
　　　　　These are invisible matters which matter.
How can we find a balance between duty and desire
when mass Media competes for every second of our attention?
Both Poles melt fast dissolving mother earth and
greed succeeds carrying GMO seeds.
Species eliminated erosion explosion.
Patriarchal politics places plastic in control
vying for our time while sea life is dying
and the even meek have ceased their need for equality.

—*Susan M. Sanders, Burlington*

Before My Homeland Had a Name

it simply was.
Boulders and grime and spent seeds in the streams
breathed
with unforgiving moss, spread in silence without protest.
And when copper-brushed rains hushed thrushes into place,
I think I was born.
A name with cragged consonants too many,
uncushioned by forgiving vowels,
you, nonetheless, cradled it gently in your mouth
while you whispered your gracious years into my ear
until the hour you could no longer breathe,
and it caught, excruciatingly, in your throat.
In a desperate, deafening rasp,
you expelled me
from you,
leaving me with myself
and a name now foreign and only my own.
I perch on cliffs that hover precariously
above mercy,
from whence my ancestors
crawled
to be flooded by copper-brushed rains.

—*Kelly Sargent, Williston*
previously published in *Kitchen Table Quarterly*, January 2023

Women's Circles

The Mothers and Grandmothers
live in my kitchen
Their circles
are plates and bowls
Their talking stick
a slotted spoon
used for gesturing and
mixing together the ingredients of our lives.

—Nancy Scarcello, Florence

That Old Story

That old story, you know the one,
where you're wearing the gnarled sheepskin
    and everything, tucked neatly beneath,
        blood type O
        ovarian cyst
        OCD
    Everything unseen is unseemly.
You know that story—
you lived it.
    When a sleepy game of Chutes and Ladders
    could collapse into swirling and slipping,
    water glass smashing the wall,
    leather belt snapping on buttocks.
When the one in charge of reassurance
was too busy swimming upstream in a shark-infested mind
    trap
        hating your smell,
        your will,
        your mind's canyons,
        your heart's parched garden,
        your concentrated form,
            a can of drippy frosted purple juice
            in desperate need of water,
            a container,
            and four glasses to share.

—*Gail Marlene Schwartz, Montpelier*

The Door

Chaos
grime...grime...grime
anxiety grips
fatigue
door closes
Darkness

Disentanglement
time...time...time
misty morning dawn
door opens
anxiety flies
peace
Light

—*Rachel Senechal, East Montpelier*

July Fever

The summer the city was sick,
it heaved its organs onto the street.
We brought shovels
and waded thigh-high in mud boots
to scrape filth from the sidewalks
and silt from its lungs.

The summer the city was sick,
we strung pipes through the windows
and pumped air through its shoddy frame;
a make-shift ventilator
kicking up dust.

The summer the city was sick,
we bundled its body in canvas,
and soothed it
an infant, red with fever
and still it cried.

The summer the city was sick,
we told it stories.
We've been here too,
we said,
we'll wait.

—*Aurora Sharp, Moretown*

29 October 2023

I Reach Out—from that sometime golden fantasy of
    self-sufficiency that surrounds me.

I Reach Out—to what I deem unworthy and begin to
    co-create peace.

I Would Reach Out—to the now of that woman I shy
    away from.
 She glances at me with fear and self-loathing,
as she threads a grocery cart—empty—through the
    pedestrian crowd on Main Street.

I Would Reach In—to that love-resisting stone inside my heart.
I yearn to shatter it—and use its fragments to bridge the void
between me and that woman.
For she is one among a multitude of Wondrous Divine
    Manifestations
I have been taught to ignore.

I might say to her:
Perhaps there is something you need I can give you, and
    something I need you might give me.

Can I accept that interdependency between me and thee?

                I am because you are.

—L V M Shelton, Montpelier

Ways We Like Onion River Outdoors!

Onion River outdoors.
New stuff every week.
Inspiring to all.
OUTDOORS.
Number one in our book.
River of the wild onions.
Very adventurous.
In Montpelier, Vermont.
East State St.
Really friendly.

—Helen Shoesmith, age 9, Montpelier

Something to rise

take it as it's given the rain and then
a beaming blue horizon the geese I didn't
hear and the bear waking to the black

oil seeds we left for the wild turkey lord
what fools we ask for spring and then
deal with the consequences the peaches

blushing in the grocery store out of season
we don't need a reason to bake a cake
just the urge the eggs flour and milk

something to rise I am lonely for the geese
and the snow falling yesterday was a sign

get up open up make something of it all

—Rebecca Siegel, Thetford Center

Watch/Warning/Flood

I admit it—
I went to get a coffee
So I could see how high
The water was...this time

I stood on the bridge
Next to the people with their Wilaiwan bowls
Next to the newspaper people
Next to the kids out early from school
Looking across to the watchers
On the Langdon Street bridge
Looking back at us

I walked slowly back to the library
The granite
Dark gray
From all the rain
And I checked my desk drawers
To make sure there wasn't anything
I couldn't bear to lose,
Just in case

—*Michelle A.L. Singer, East Montpelier*

Reflections While Fishing

I've been fishing, mostly,
in dirty rivers:

plugged, polluted,
plodding like prose.

Old pals, repeatedly,
text and send images:

mountains and trout,
and crystal, clear streams.

Pure poetry, they say,
searching for praise.

I delete and go about my day:

casting, continuously,
onto a muddy surface,

wistful that, someday,
something will rise.

—*Grant Smith, Montpelier*

Beech

A connection so strong
that even as its jade fades,
and its skin pales and folds
and curls around bended ribs,
the link does not break
between leaf and limb,
not in ice storms or blizzards
when whole Maples, Basswoods and
Ash were made bare months before.

What explanation I ask
of the Beech
That there is beauty in aging?
Yes, that is true, but perhaps
there's a wizardry beneath
the blonde curls rattling
in frozen winds.
Its new buds are veiled
from hungry deer.

—*Martha E. Snell, El Cerrito, California*

Nothing in Nature is Simple

Consider the roots of Junipers—
bent, twisted, sunk into pale sand
down to the secret depths of water,
the branches bare of foliage and berries
and shedding fibers of brown skin.
They are not dead, they drink.
At the surface they play
with shadows of light
that arc, angle and sustain.
The gamut of life.

—*Martha E. Snell, El Cerrito, California*

The Wonder

Imagine that you can cling onto crystals,
wedge one foot then the other
into hexagonal corners,
grasp the edges of glassy spans,
and climb   hand-over-hand
up cubic ladders of close-packed crystals
like topaz, tanzanite or celestite.

At the top you will sit   steady yourself   breathe
then gaze out into space   to see
the forever past, the faint ancient lights
of stars and galaxies, though just
a sampling with your only-human eyes.
You will hear silence, but you will know
there are booming sounds of breaking and making.

—*Martha E. Snell, El Cerrito, California*

When You Visit

the museum of knees
entering through architectures
of cartilage and ligament
        You will see walls covered
with icons of genuflection
before the feared
ōor the revered.
        You may not recognize
your bones in devotion
your muscles in contraction.
        You may not recognize
yourself in the inner circles
of countries or cultures
of despots and autocrats.
        You may not recognize
yourself in the outer circles
of the mislaid and expendable
fodder for fabrications and philosophies, wars.
        You may not recognize my bent back
with all the awestruck children folding before
caregivers, churches, institutions, ideologies that
stand for a lifetime and sparkle too long over us.

—*sb sōwbel, Montpelier*

Working Mother

The most efficient
thing can be to stop
and listen, to take hold of your hand—
but look at this desk
piles of to-do lists and no air between them

You are old enough to say
            I just want to be with you

When only a few years ago you stumbled
over consonants
You cried instead of spoke
And I'd sweep you up then,
as if pressing our cheeks together could
fix the world

Was it true for you?
Was that all it took?
I just want to take care
of you, and so I work

But you look at me as if
this is backward
as if taking care
is what works

—*Katie Spring, Worcester*

Blues for the Masses

Honoring Reuben Jackson

Remember when our intelligence
was a thing?
Remember that?
Remember when Human Intelligence
was the ticket to moving forward
when wisdom won the race
when that which separates
a bad road from a good road
was one's ability to align the stars
and go?
Remember when Human Intelligence
discovered things
built things
solved things
answered things
wrote things
sang things
moved things
summoned things
believed things
loved things
that otherwise seemed impossible?
Remember when Human Intelligence
was a thing?
When the smartest way forward
was your own?

—*Toussaint St. Negritude, Newark*

Together

small bodies that clustered together
bound to have features in common,
heaved and bubbled gigantically
in constant complicated motion.

they fell together and together
the two go dancing off
to penetrate the mysteries
that forces them apart.

before they could meet again,
an even more intimate connection
accomplished–superbly–
vaster in scope than ever before.

mutual gravitational attraction
is the nature of all these curious things,
each has a story to tell
before they disappear.

—*Heather Stearns, White River Junction*

Prescient

My mother murmured into the phone—
She knew everything
but couldn't go to the pharmacy
because the pharmacist read her mind.

Her doctor sent her to the hospital.
We visited her in the atrium
and ate on linen tablecloths.

Reason took center stage for a moment.
She saw us as though standing on us,
eyes stuffed with glass.

—*Samn Stockwell, Barre*
from *Musical Figures*, Thirty West Publishing House

Water, Life's Partner!

Falling from the sky,
On to its' demise or future,
As if borne from the womb,
Reaching, connecting, touching, forming...

Just falling...
Softly, hard, all at once,
Dancing with the wind,
With the forces that dictate...
Its' place and function in the moment...

Clouds let their cargo go downward,
The amount joined by its' volume and weight...
Water, can be life, death, salvation, destruction.
    Rivers, ponds, lakes, oceans, soil...
Everything alive... all depend on it.

Cycle goes on... water transformed from beneath,
Evaporates moving upward,
Creating clouds that become pregnant
And then let go... free...

From then on,
It is downwards where drops of liquid
Have different outcomes...
Water is life's incredible partner!

—*Yvonne Straus, Montpelier*

Ode to a Lioness

I honestly don't think she'd want to rest in peace, even in
    death, while there is still
injustice in the world.
So Rage On, Lioness, Rage on!

Your words still incite riots for justice.
The Truth is still heard ringing in your voice, clear &
    vibrant like an everlasting torrent,
Raging down the halls of justice, Roaring to be heard,
Pounding on the doors of politicians as you rage on,
Demanding to be enacted in laws to protect & lift up the
    oppressed!
Rage On, Lioness, Rage On!

Crazy, they said.
You were mad & so am I!
Mad as Hell & We're Not Gonna Take It Anymore!
We're All Mad Here.
Rage On, Lioness, Rage On!

You shaved your mane, and became even more of a Lioness,
More powerful & hungry for truth & justice,
And more skilled at hunting down & exposing the sinew &
    bone of liars than even the
strongest Maned Lion.
So Rage on, Lioness, Rage on!

No time for meter, not the season for rhyme; these are my
    words from my heart, for a
woman who helped inspire the Lioness in Me, because the
    Lion & the Cobra helped

teach me to ROAR.
Rage on, Sinead, Rage on!

—*Ashley Anne Strobridge* | *Astrobridge Artistry, Montpelier*

Orchard

The absurdity of it
standing in lines
offering fistfuls of shiny fruit
gnarled by sheer abundance
whispering a startling history
each apple a flower
each tree a seed
that repeats
row after row.

I thank you by name
as time permits
red delicious, macintosh
pink lady, gala, honey crisp

but soon baskets overflow
twisted branches offer a spot to sit and eat.

Bees hum among the fallen
pressed to cider beneath our soles
and like Eve
I cannot consider
a life without apples.

—*Lynn Parrish Sutton, Burlington*

Beginning with One Stone

First, I have to
stop
notice
start small
this tear-drop-shaped stone
on the path.
Bending down,
I gently turn it over
two rollie pollies curl into balls,
returning me to childhood
hand flat with rollie pollies stretching
then curling
under my touch.

A small brown spider walks
over leaves
disappears
I wait
watch.

Today, I look out
on the snow-covered landscape
I know
there is more
underneath.

—*Pamela Tallmadge, Colchester*

Haiku: snow and ice

I open my eyes:
snow and ice cover the world—
I will dream again

—*Geza Tatrallyay, Barnard*

Dreaming Sky

Once, when we were young, we tried to fly
With stunted cedar bows clutched in our small hands
Their needles pricking instantly at our bare scrawny arms
Twisted and one much larger than the other, heavy, clunky
Nothing like the wind-hearted feathers we had tried to
    emulate, but wings nonetheless
We thought we were brilliant, we believed, truly
That we would soar with our mismatched contraptions
We dreamed such big dreams
Once
Then we ran, flinging ourselves down that hill
Flailing our enlarged arms
And trying, desperately to catch the sky
Tripping, tumbling, Jumping a little as we went, refusing to
    let go of that hope
That dream to join the swallows in their azure domain
We didn't fly, of course we didn't, but does it matter ?
Because we were still standing there
Wingless creatures forever bound to earth gazing up at the
    blue blue sky
And I wonder now
Do I still dare to dream? Would I still throw myself down
    that looming slope?
Today
Without hesitation
Would I still wish, would I still try
I wonder now
Can I still fly?

—*Ella Thomas, Calais*

Secret

found poem: source text: Fahrenheit 451, *Ray Bradbury*

With eyes so dark
a phoenix was
walking in a circle in the Moonlight.
I have a suspicion
that he had read a forbidden book.

—*Leilah Thompson, Cabot*

Now

Long white hair wears blue
With friendly agreement
A ribbon a bow a band around
Blue never worked before now

Cobalt eyes twinkle
With crinkles around each
Natural lashes are few
Noticed with cosmetic help

Wardrobe settled on black
Simple without comment
Highlighting the blue above
Covering a widened girth

Metallic blue trucks cruise
The sky reveals cerulean
Beneath debris oceans
Hope for azure and teal

Singing the blues out loud
With no one to listen
Now moving seductively
Into the kitchen for tea

—TT Tomlinson, Essex Junction

Twice

A greeting card once taught me,
      Truly Taught me
The secret every poet needs
              —really needs—

On every line
     repeat a word
            twice
      The last word twice.

Instant rhyme!
     Gratifying rhyme!

My problem is,
         sadly is,
When I say, I love you
     I cannot stop at two,
        stop at two.

I love you
     I love you
I love you...
     You know who

—*Robert Troester, Montpelier*

Noise canceling

I can still hear my heart in silence
in the quiet, its beats are the loudest thing.
They're steady and when I focus on them
get faster

like footsteps. Walking, solid, advancing, running.
I take a breath to quiet them, the stomps.
My heart is chasing me from a ribcage drum.

It's a cell phone in a bowl when you don't have
a speaker, I'm trying frantically to adjust the bass.

"Be still," I say silently to this organ,
this Thwomp of increasing speeds, but
there's no shushing this time as it
grows ever larger in my mind,
threatening a heart takeover,
disquieting a body.

I'm not listening. I actively ignore the
blood coursing in time and think
of irregular things, imagine a wind chime,
crave a truck releasing its air brakes,
would do anything for a song.

—*Tamsen Turner, East Calais*

Reaching Ken

Sometimes the door between rooms simply locks
but we still have that crack underneath.

Won't you lie on your belly
with me
and see if we can make our fingers meet?

—Betsy Unger, Montpelier

ken

(n) - one's range of grasp, knowledge, or sight

(v) - to recognize, to know

The Guest Book

Page after page of handwritten names—
parties, overnight guests, drop-ins

Gem from '99: "Emergency Ice Cream-Eating-Party"
friends who rallied when our freezer died

Wedding, baby showers, graduations—
just like that, filled cover to cover

Like a new-car smell, soft suede
volume awaits travelers, fun times

Only entry was late 2019—elegant cursive
Cousins Steve and Miyo on their way to Montreal

Blank pages follow, guest book shelved—
month after month when no one came to stay

—*Candelin Wahl, Burlington*

Reverse Heroics

Nearing the put-in on the Allagash
we were two happy couples in a car
my guy and two old friends
the canoes traveling along on the top

In conversation the other man had muttered to me,
"I wouldn't want you in my fox hole."
Oh, I think of battlefields and heroics
purpose and specially trained abilities

Off we went, John and wife venturing before us
facing glorious, wild gushing white water
with trusty dog Mo, and the wannigan full
of lunch, beer, and my fresh chocolate chip cookies

I in the stern of our beloved green Old Town
judging, calculating, measuring, watching
the heady joy of adventure, maybe danger
but knowing the importance of choice

Over into the brink crashed our brave soldier
grabbing over rocks, the overturned canoe gone
he, then soaking on the shore, incoherent, hypothermic
I, safely downstream, preferring my own private fox hole

—*Janet Watton, Randolph Center*

Two Roberts

I found myself in your snowy wood
as a very young child.
It was in my blood. In the late '40s,
your train companion from Cleveland
to New York spoke little English,
but you made each other understood,
and the world has not yet known of the 30
original personal annual handwritten
Christmas poems to your friend,
my grandfather, held in my mother's care.
Of course, I ended up in Vermont—a poet.
Another Robert reaches out across time
via Van Gogh and Bernini with a pathos
that has winged away in a kaleidoscope of pain.
Where the other biographers
lash the creators with scorpion tongues,
you, Professor Wallace, wrap your artists
in a wisdom of kind understanding,
and a mastery of generous context,
shared freely—a balm across ether
where nothing seems free anymore.
Of course, you wrote of mystically-abundant
creators who flew the wonder of the world
into paint and stone, constructing my future.

—JC Wayne | *Creative for Good, Charlotte*

Black Birds

you're a clutter
of black feathered cups, a squawk
of comments, all dark
flutter and fluff, you sit
at the tips of stripped winter trees. Moving,
you amuse me. Puff
and puff, awk! awk! awk!
I salute your squeaky pulse
while you turn
and dance
just in time.

—Sharon Webster, Burlington
from *O Song*, forthcoming from Salmon Poetry

Cathedral

Aquarian sun blazes off the snowpack
blinding me with birdsong,
blue skies and change.

Every year I make a pact
with darkness.

I surrender to the season,
bed down with animals,
eat red meat and chocolate

clad in layers of wool.
But here it is again—sunlight

on my face in the windless
meadow. Actual heat,

not the polar queen's bitter gaze.
A flock of wild turkeys
scores its three-pronged tracks

like runes for me to trace
into the forest. I didn't know
I was waiting for a sign.

In the cathedral of pines
a rough arch, a gold shadow,
the red walls of my heart

expanding in snow.

—*Diana Whitney, Brattleboro*

Creation

When we were young
Spindles on the back staircase
Were post office boxes

And I fed our father's junk mail
Through the slats
In some way that made sense
To my child's mind

Sorting and grouping by
Size or color
But never by
Sender or purpose.

When I look at you now
I want to smooth
The wrinkled edges of
Your enveloped face.

When I look at you now
I wish I still had the power
To bring order out of chaos.

—*Emily A. Wills, Fairfax*

Tree of Life

Afterschool memories sheltered on the porch
Under a tree bough from the sun
Dreaming of tomorrow and feeling timeless
Those days seem so providential

I see evergreen and believe I'm still there
When things were so simple and fun
When things seemed carefree, and life was such a bliss
Oh, what a joy to be fearless

I stand firm as a pine, though my needles shake
Thirty rings to remember all
Those memories taste sweet, like sumac berries
The mistakes rough as crackling leaves

Even as winter has shed my resolve and
Left me bare to prevaricate
I know spring will arrive soon, and buds will form
And graft new memories for me

I can see I am the scion of my ancestors
Creating a new stock from it
Prescinding from the nodes I had blossomed from,
Making seasons evanescent

—*M. Wilson, Barre*

When the Second Person Dies*

Certain losses change your grammar.
"You" disappears. "She" arrives.

To never again say to the beloved
"You have spinach in your teeth,
  that tee shirt matches your eyes today,
  your sunglasses are on top of the piano."

What remains are those glasses she
was looking for, the piano, that shirt
in her closet, the desperation to say aloud
"Hi you, welcome home, I love you."

—Heather Wishik, Woodstock
*from "My Mother" by Victoria Chang

Cirrostratus

Why, O' gallant beast,
O' servant and served of nature,
well molded epiphany of god,
denier of earthly laws and conjunctions,
do you taunt me so? How dare
you float in vapid peace,
in tangled aberration,
smiling with suckling glee,
eked out from nothing but spare sputum?
They call you inspiration
and yet this rasp upon my eyes
feels more like damnation!
I call you liar among majesty,
sickness amongst not but a new babe,
Beelzebub! Let me lie
in my woe, for I am bare
against the whims of mother,
and her thousand furious lashes
against my clock.

—*Shyloh Wonder-Maez, Barre*

Transient Breath

When the full white moon
of a mid-winter's night
pours—black shadows
on a crystalline forest floor
life is pressed—firmly
against a thick cold silence
 then
life may be seen
as the rhythmic transient breath
of one—standing alone
beneath a steady starlit sky.

—James W. Wyman, Alburgh

Among Canards

Lord love a duck! As well as why-not entertain
a she-mallard's own scurrilous antics as ill-reputed
as mine, her beady-eyed & feather-
headed immodesties & her since-when nobody
listens not even another poultry. You could please
flip us a couple of yesteryears' raggedy toast crusts.

I'll preen my own rear wag,
showing myself off shabby in plain
oversight & scuffling such scrappy disinformations & tattles
as everywhere drop along behind cripple
winter now so mildly driven-off however
spittling & muttering yesterday.

This, that: my current trumpsed-up undeniably not
among the notions I held in mind high-&-mightily
once-upon-time, none amounting to much, but today,
addled yet, I keep keen & nimble enough
to tip up & dabble, muckster still of any pond's black heart
beneath the superficial clouds swaggering upside-down like
     luck

—*Martha Zweig, Hardwick*
previously published in *Cider Press Review*, vol. 23, issue 2

Schools

Calais Elementary School: Samantha Jackson's Third and Fourth Grade Class

Candy

candy is sour, candy is sweet
it is a very good treat
there are many different kinds
of candy like Starburst
and Gummy Worms

—Lillian B., Grade 3, Calais Elementary School

Happiness

Happiness is when you are with your friends and having fun.
Also, it feels good when you have good games
have good times with your friends

Having good food
Happiness is good.

—Maddi B., Grade 4, Calais Elementary School

Snow

Soft and fluffy flakes fall from the sky,
No sign of the sun all day and all night,
On the ground lies a blanket of cold and white snow,
Which crunches like paper wherever you go.

—Sam B., Grade 3, Calais Elementary School

Book

A book is a book
you are you
anything is what
they want to be
just like how
A book is a book

—Maggie C., Grade 3, Calais Elementary School

Loneliness

It feels like long lost puppy
It looks like a stray dog
It smells like a canine left in the rain
It tastes like rotten dog food
It sounds like the howl like a sad puppy

—*Frances E., Grade 4, Calais Elementary School*

Leaves

Leaves are soft and colorful
In the fall I play in piles
The sounds excite me
Relaxes me and calms me
As I lay down in it
I feel enjoyment
I smile happy
I don't want to leave it.

—*Lennox F., Grade 4, Calais Elementary School*

Leaves

The leaves on trees
They came and now
they're gone.
But don't be upset
in the spring
the leaves
will come back.

—Liam F., Grade 3, Calais Elementary School

Family

Fun
Awesome
Mine
Involved
Loving
Yours

—Derek G., Grade 4, Calais Elementary School

Clock

The clock is on the wall
It goes around and around
It copies itself ticks and ticks
When I walk into a room
I see a clock and I wonder
What it is like to be a
Clock it just hangs
On the wall
Like at school
You just sit.

—*Ella G., Grade 4, Calais Elementary School*

My Device

I am using a device I use it twice I use it thrise and it is colored like butter I wonder how I can see it it is dark as the night after the sunset I play family games as fun as the rain I just want a main to show to this device I want to see its full potential but nope some sites are out of order so I sit here and wait for the night just to come back and search for the creature to show its light oh this device just showed itself twice thrice frice fithe and it goes on and on but thats just the beginning of the story you can be nice to my device but I just want more sights to look at night but once the sunrise comes up once twice through centuries millenniums aras for infinite years through new galaxies worlds lifetimes say high to time to all the colors through these galaxies and worlds all these colors flashing through time oh I wish I could see such a sight oh this device please come show me.

—Joseph G., Grade 4, Calais Elementary School

Champion

He shoots he scores oh whata goal
that was to tie
fantastic goal I don't know what to say
I could just go hooray
this is just wack
ohhh whata hack
this time not hooray
this time it's booray
but we're tied
we're headed up with speed
5,4,3,2,1 errrrrrr there goes the buzzer
we scored another
oh whata show

—William G., Grade 4, Calais Elementary School

Happiness

Happiness is compliments from friends.
And is Zelda.
It is having fun with my friends.
Eating pizza with my mom and dad.
Swimming in Curtis Pond with my friends.
Reading with my mom and dad.
Happiness is getting a new pet.
Doing social studies at school.
Snuggling with my pets.
Happiness.

—Finn K., Grade 3, Calais Elementary School

Livy

Loves family
Is a human
Very kind
Yes, this is very real

—Livy L., Grade 3, Calais Elementary School

Silliness

Silliness is the color green it makes you laugh
It tastes like a sour apple it smells like candy

It sounds like laughter.

—Astrid M., Grade 4, Calais Elementary School

Leaves

leaves of
color falling down,
leaves of color all around.
leaves leaves everywhere,
watch your cat swat them
out there.

—Colin O., Grade 4, Calais Elementary School

Guilt

Guilt makes you feel bad

And connects you to feel anxious.

Guilt can help you get better at things.

Guilt feels like losing something on accident

And you get a huge blame.

Guilt tastes bitter like you just

Brushed your teeth and drank orange juice.

Guilt smells like burnt rubber and makes you mad.

—*Shepherd P., Grade 3, Calais Elementary School*

Petals

A thousand petals
dancing all around us, swirl
twirl, all around us

—Odessa R., Grade 3, Calais Elementary School

Loneliness

It feels like a puppy that got kicked out of the group.
It looks like a rainbow that never gets shown.
It tastes like rotten canine food.

It smells like a puppy that has a broken heart.
It sounds like a sad dog howling.
Loneliness is the color gray.

—Elia S., Grade 4, Calais Elementary School

Mad

Mad looks like a crackling fire
Mad is the color red
Mad smells like burning wood
Mad taste like a hot red pepper
Mad feels like an inferno inside.

—Hazel S., Grade 3, Calais Elementary School

The Car

It is a vehicle
It has a motor
It hauls people
It goes really fast
It goes really far

—Ryan S., Grade 3, Calais Elementary School

Love

Laughter
Over loved
Valuable
Extra

—Emma W., Grade 3, Calais Elementary School

Sleepy

Sleepy makes me angry in the morning.
Sleepy makes me hungry.
Sleepy makes me tired.
Sleepy makes me want to go to bed.
Sleepy tastes like eating peanut butter.

—Owen W., Grade 4, Calais Elementary School

Trees

Trees bending in wind
Trees bend in multiple ways
Trees give us cool shade

—Andrew Z., Grade 4, Calais Elementary School

Main Street Middle School, Montpelier:
Kiki Adams's Fifth Grade Class

Life

Living
Alive, Fun
Breathing, feeling, playing
They're alive and then they're gone
Rotting, freezing, fading
Sadness, regret
Death

—*Freya A.-M., Grade 5, Main Street Middle School*

War

Screams and gunshots filled every town,
People had built bunkers to try and stay safe.
They failed.
No one,
And nowhere was safe.
My mother and I were trying to escape,
We were almost out of site,
Almost safe.
But then the sounds of boots followed
Behind us.
We ran faster,
The boots grew closer.
BAM!
Dead,
Unmoving,
The two words that had described my mother that moment.
I kept running,
I held back tears,
I couldn't end up like her,
No,
I refused to end up like that.
BAM!
A sharp pain nailed me in the back,
I collapsed.
And now I to was dead,
And unmoving,
Just like my mother.

—*Louisa F., Grade 5, Main Street Middle School*

Music Is A Rhyme

Music is a rhyme
The pattern stays there all the time
You can never let it go
Once the rhythm's touched your heart
This poem is to let you know
That rhymes keep going from the start

—Charlotte G., Grade 5, Main Street Middle School

New to you

It's love,
Soft like a dove,
Burning bright.

Your stomach is turning,
Your palms are burning,
It's love.

—Iris K., Grade 5, Main Street Middle School

Gardening

Gardening
Beam, Gleam
Weeding, Growing, Knowing
Spring will come any day now—
Do not forget me, Forget-me not's
Show your face up high in the sky.
Never mind, I've lost my mind, Spring is not today.
Nobody Knows, when you'll grow—
So I will wait. Wow, that's great
You've already decided to grow!
Slowly, Slowly, Growing
There's your face!
Gardening

—Theo K., Grade 5, Main Street Middle School

Hummingbirds

You buzz like a bee
You enjoy sugar water
You are very pretty

—Charlotte R., Grade 5, Main Street Middle School

Nature

I hear noise
Crickets, birds, raindrops
The world in the forest
This is my home
This is where I belong
I see foxes playing
Squirrels are gathering acorns
Wolves are hunting for deer
This is the world I long for
Peace and quiet
This is me

—Isabella R., Grade 5, Main Street Middle School

My Cat's Eyes

My cat's eyes are like emeralds,
She can jump up to the sky,
Her paws are cotton balls,
And her name is Gem, just like her eyes

—Freya S., Grade 5, Main Street Middle School

Main Street Middle School, Montpelier:
Debbie Goodwin's Sixth Grade Class

Queer Equality

They think my thoughts are wrong.
They think my existence is illegal.
Just because my view of
The world isn't the same as theirs.
They stop me from being who I am.
We were blamed for something that nobody
Had control over, because of people's nonsense
Opinions. You may see, hear, and sense how sad the world is,
You might also ignore it.
Some called us gross, some called us sins.
Nothing can stop what this world thinks of us,
Because the past, and the future, can't always make things better.
Awful, discriminatory people will always be here,
no matter how hard we try.
but that doesn't mean we should stop trying
to make the world better.

—*Anonymous, Grade 6, Main Street Middle School*

Starry Nights

I love really starry nights
Stars take my focus away
Love the way they shine
There are quadrillions of stars in the sky

Twinkles in the sky
Shining brightly
Can't stop looking at them
It's like they are racing far away from me so I can't catch
    them easily.

Teasing and taunting with their beautiful shine
I wonder if they look like the sun.

—*Anonymous, Grade 6, Main Street Middle School*

Basketball

Orange with black stripes
Shiny like a golden ring
With a rough texture

Times of happiness
Freedom from horrendous school
Ball bouncing around,

Fun to play with now
How I wish I could right now
Play the greatest game

—*Adim B., Grade 6, Main Street Middle School*

Weeping Willow

Green with glory the Monster Size willow tree.
Wisteria blossoms under the impact of a bumble bee.
The chipmunks and squirrels love the wild raspberries sweet.
Sets the sun, Rises the moon goddess that blesses the land
   with glowing standers.
She grants a loon a wish of voice and her goal is done. While
   the animals hear
the singing and ringing they have a fall to slumber

                    Goodnight sweet willow tree

—EL C., Grade 6, Main Street Middle School

She Does

A small songbird sits on a branch, singing to me with its
soulful song, who values this
small speck of life?
She does, she does with her kind heart, she does with her
gentle hands, she does,
she helps those birds with their injured wings,
with their broken talons, as she wraps, stitches, and then,
sets them free,
"Goodbye," she says as they spread their wings and soar
through the warm brightly
colored autumn leaves never looking back,
and she just watches,
She does, she does, she does.

—*Molly C., Grade 6, Main Street Middle School*

The Dancer of the Sky

A parrot dances in the sky
Like a dancer in the Nutcracker
Reaching the ground
Its colors swirling
Landing on a moss covered branch for a rest.

Then it spread its wings to fly
Taking off into the sky
For its next adventure awaits it.
Its destination is Far
So It prepares itself for a long fly

—Natalie F., Grade 6, Main Street Middle School

Fire & Water

Fire
Red, Hot, Blaze
Blazing, Burning, Roaring
As hot as the sun
Still warm like a blanket

Water
Blue, Cool, Calm
Dripping, Flooding, Flowing
As cold as the winds of Antarctica
Still refreshing like a bottle of Fiji water

—Karthi J., Grade 6, Main Street Middle School

Waves

The waves crashing
With a lot of trash
The ones who dumped with a lot of cash
See, see
Do something now
No? Ok. Get ready to see the end

The heat rising like a rocket ship flying
The cold falling like a meteorite crashing
Now will you do something?
Finally
Get ready for the truth you will uncover

—*Nimish J., Grade 6, Main Street Middle School*

Cascading River of Rain

Coming to the land,
falling in cascading sheets,
bounding,
racing its twins to the ground.
But always shifting, changing,
running away when the sun shows its rays.
Sometimes it can stay for days.

In the morning the rain goes cold,
however when the day grows old,
the rain is ice cold once more.
In mid day, she can't stay away,
from the memory of the play,
following the bright blue birds.
In fascination she gapes,
At the grapes that hang,
from the vine.
Whispering something she heard,
she does, from her hiding spot in winter, at the bird.

—Eden K., Grade 6, Main Street Middle School

A Beautiful Winter

Snowflakes are falling slowly
Covering the world in a blanket of white
A cold breeze shoots through the air
The night sky shining, the stars bright

Frosty mountains and treetops
Little sparks in the sky
Frozen like tiny raindrops
Reflecting in the cloudless blue of the night

Sitting by the fireplace
Looking longingly out the window
A light shone upon her face
Oh, how beautiful this Winter is

—*Winnie L., Grade 6, Main Street Middle School*

The Cat in May Named José

Once there was a cat that sat on my lap
I feed it so much
That it got very fat.

Meow, meow the cat will happily plead

As it simply will feed.

He was as big as a Doctor Suess
Roast beast
Beated.

The cat is a cotton ball
As the cold rain slowly went
Fall,fall,fall.

The cat lived in a small house
The house had a mouse
The cat quickly chased the mouse
In a house.

The cat hit the hay
He was next to the chimney
And the chimney was ablaze.

The name of the cat was José,
The grass was green
The cat was gray
And all this happened all in May.

—*Micah M., Grade 6, Main Street Middle School*

The Cycle

Spring, fresh, look—hummer!
Changing, growing to summer

Summer, swim, silly,
Changing, cooling down to fall

Fall, jewels far and wide,
Changing, snow piled beside

Winter, white, windy,
Changing, warming up to spring.

The Cycle
Everchanging,
Nothing to stop it.

—Abe R., Grade 6, Main Street Middle School

Vegas

Las Vegas, a city for giants
Valued ceilings in Vegas
for making bills
Towering buildings sprawling for
Blocks
miles of crossings

for bright tourist flocks

The rooms are suite,
The limos are fleet
Rivers indoors and playhouses galore
And all sorts of people to meet.

—*Saul S., Grade 6, Main Street Middle School*

Birds in Winter

Birds eating from the feeder
I watch as they scramble to get food
Red, blue, yellow and black
Doing what they need to survive harsh winter
Singing their songs

In this cold harsh winter
Never looking back

Winter is hard to survive
I watch as all their colors mix
Now they are ready for winter
They can return to their families
Every bird vanishes as they fly through the cold harsh winter
Ready for everything that could come their way

—*Evelyn W., Grade 6, Main Street Middle School*

Starry Skies

Starry skies speckled
beautiful gleaming a white—
Such amazements now

Every full night
They speckle the sky brightly
Diamond in hiding

They're singing loudly
A sweet ring ring ring ringing
Such an old habit

—*Ellison Z., Grade 6, Main Street Middle School*

Main Street Middle School, Montpelier:
Windy Kelley's Fifth Grade Class

Fire

Fire—
hot, bright
heat, light
moving, changing, growing, burning
—Fire

—*Mason B., Grade 5, Main Street Middle School*

Flood

The rain poured for days
It seeped into the ground
Water rushed in
And filled up our town

Close to spillway
Fingers crossed
Panicking and pacing
Summer fun lost

Overflowing rivers
Clogged up drains
Worrying and waiting
Tempers strained

Houses were lakes of dirty water
Everyone chipped in and lent a hand
Much was destroyed
But Montpelier did withstand

Downtown dried up
Friends helped friends
Stores reopened
We tied up loose ends

So our little town of Montpelier
Made it after all
We worked as a community
Together we stand tall

—*Marissa E.-C., Grade 5, Main Street Middle School*

Time

Time.
Always moving forward.
Stone walls crumble to the ground.
Wood darkens and dicares.

Moss grows and dies.
Vines hang peacefully from the trees.
Water carves channels in stone cliffs.
Birds chirp peacefully unaware of the passing of time.

Sprouts grow into strong trees.
Leaves light up with the colors of fire.
Birds fly south for winter.
Life moves forward with the passing of time.

—Isabelle K., Grade 5, Main Street Middle School

Blue

Roses are red, violets are blue
I help you when the moon is blue.
:D :D :D

—Kira L., Grade 5, Main Street Middle School

The Evergreen Forest

The sacramento green ferns
And flower buds opening
Sun light raining down
On the hard forest floor

Chipmunks scatter
As the hawk over head
Gets ready to dive
Hungry for it's well-earned meal

The many colors
Bright and beautiful
Pastels and Bolds
Greens, reds, blues, and yellows

Birds chirp to each other
Asking about one another's day
Communicating in a secret language
That only they can understand

Leaves slowly, gracefully falling
In heaps and piles
Ready to be reborn
Just in time for Spring

The towering pine trees
Swaying in the gentle winds
That race through
The Evergreen Forest

—*Layla M., Grade 5, Main Street Middle School*

Nighttime

Nighttime, so peaceful
so quiet,
and yet, so loud.
Hear the crickets chirping,
the wind whistling,
The nighttime is wonderful.

—Beatrice P., Grade 5, Main Street Middle School

Spring

The warm breeze rustles leaves
Green grass shows under melting snow
Birds chirp in budding trees
Streams trickle down mountains
Bright sun shines through puffy clouds

—Alvida S., Grade 5, Main Street Middle School

Four Seasons

Birds are chirping.
All is wonderful.
It is raining.
It is blazing.
It is blinding.
It is beautiful.
It is Grainy.
It is falling.
It is snowing.
The day is so full.
It is snowy.
The year is coming to a ending.

—Jacoby S., Grade 5, Main Street Middle School

Seasons

So many blossoms and flowers
You are walking past those flowers and blossoms
Birds chirping sweet melody
It's Spring and It's just starting

The sun is shining and people are swimming
Swatches of ice cream on the sidewalk that fell from
people's melted
ice-cream
It's Summer and it's warm

Leaves are falling from trees
You feel a cool breeze past your face
A leave falls on your head
It's Fall and leaves are falling

Snow is everywhere and everything is white
You are walking on the snowy sidewalk
A snowflake falls on your nose
It's Winter and it's coming for you

—Naira V., Grade 5, *Main Street Middle School*

Dogs and Shoes

I told you to stop chewing on my shoes
Then you War war in the Blues
Then you decided to take a snooze
When you woke up I said I have some bad news
I said please don't chew on my shoes.

—Christian W., Grade 5, Main Street Middle School

When I Am Older

When I am older
I will go to a game
Of American football
I will clap and cheer
And buy a beer
And a bag of popcorn too
But right now I'm stuck with school lunch
(Which sometimes looks like goo)
If only I was older

—Jolyon W., Grade 5, Main Street Middle School

Main Street Middle School, Montpelier:
Wendy McGuiggan's Fifth Grade Class

Sweaters

Sweaters are cozy
When you're inside on a cold night.
They make sure your never rosey
And they'll keep you all right.

—Eloise (Ellie) A., Grade 5, Main Street Middle School

When the Sun Sets

When the field is tired it stops
When the soldiers charge they roar
When swords clash
They also bash
When the battle is done
They celebrate the sun

—Chandler B., Grade 5, Main Street Middle School

Water

Flowing, streaming
Splashing, leaping
As bright as a diamond in the sun
Jumping, spraying
Wild and playing
All currents thinking as one

—Eliza B., Grade 5, Main Street Middle School

Winter

Snowflakes falling on the ground

Covering the world with white

Without making any sound

Filling up the world with light.

—Lucille Juniper Dorwart C., Grade 5, Main Street Middle School

Fear

On one starry night
There was a fright
Like a lion both big and bright
And then he saw to his surprise
A great big pair of starry eyes
Then as he crept nearer
He saw a ... mirror

—Remy H., Grade 5, Main Street Middle School

Chance's hair

Chance's long, luscious, locks
sway in the wind,
like a plastic bag in the ocean.

—Natalie K., Grade 5, Main Street Middle School

Spring Blossoms

Daisies, light and white like snow
Tulips fill the area, bright and joyful
Pretty purple violets pack the wide fields as buzzing bumble
    bees float in

—*Chance N., Grade 5, Main Street Middle School*

School Life

The feeling of going to school and the lunch that looks like
a dead fly, I wish that I packed my own lunch, the school
work on paper, it looks weird that it's gibberish, it's funny
when you see that a toddler wrote on it but the feeling of
getting home, no work, no bad food just relaxing after
horrible school.

—*Jack N., Grade 5, Main Street Middle School*

Halloween

Owls singing softly at night
Looking at you
Owls swooping bye without a sound of fright
Swooping bye you and you after all

A scarecrow dancing off a leg
Into the unknown of the dead
Then crawling out without a sound
All wrapped up in wight and blue or dead

Black cat softly growling at night
Waking up the dead at night
Midnight
Eyes shine brightly at you made a mistake

When you wake up you find yourself
Staring at the dead as if a love story passed

Dark stares into your eyes like a
Never ending hallway with no light
Slip and slide like a toddler on a slide
then die

—*Eliana O., Grade 5, Main Street Middle School*

Restless Night

The leaves dance on silent wings, uncovering the ground
The stars shown as bright as diamonds lighting the world
    around
The thunder booms
The angry cloud looms.

The squirrels chitter
The creatures skitter
The moon whisps away
And now it's time to finally start the day.

                Oh what a restless night

—Helen P., Grade 5, Main Street Middle School

Jimmy

Jimmy is as fat as a whale
Munch! Munch! Crunch! Crunch!
Now his food is all gone
He licks his fur, Meow!
As he asks for more.

    I love Jimmy.

—Lila P., Grade 5, Main Street Middle School

Crisp morning air
Fog hovers over the lake
A loon wails from the opposite shore
Getting me full awake

I smell breakfast
Cooking on the grill
The sun will soon arise
Taking away the chill

—*Mai Huynh P., Grade 5, Main Street Middle School*

Waterfall

Rushing
Gushing
Running
Splashing
Crashing
Waterfall

—*Dex R., Grade 5, Main Street Middle School*

The Basement

I shudder in fear,
and open the door,
who knows
who knows
what hides below.

I turn on the light,
it does not take away my fright,
one step in,
two steps in,
who knows
who knows
what hides below.

I'm at the bottom,
cold cement under my feet,
the laundry basket I hold,
shakes from my unease,
I hurry,
I put
the dirty clothes in,
and start the machine,
while shivering,
who knows
who knows
what hides below.

Once it has started,
I take the laundry basket
and run,
to the steps,
don't forget to turn off the light,
out of the basement,
safe again,
because,
who knows
who knows
what hides below.

—*Edith T., Grade 5, Main Street Middle School*

The Spanish Dane

There was a great dane from spain
The great dane had no brain
He weighed ten grams
And owned twenty lambs
Then he had some pain that poor great dane

—*Owen T., Grade 5, Main Street Middle School*

Darby

Darby is kind
Darby is soft like a sheep's wool
Darby smells great
Darby's bark is soothing like the waves of the ocean
Darby's fur does not taste good

—*Zak T., Grade 5, Main Street Middle School*

Swinter

winter
white, fluffy
puffing, being, snowing
dead silence, chirping birds
biking, running, swimming
happy, sweaty
summer

—*Kasper W., Grade 5, Main Street Middle School*

Main Street Middle School, Montpelier:
Melissa Parker's Fifth Grade Class

Hunting Cat

Silent paws on ground
Ears and whiskers twitch forward
Pounce! I catch a mouse.

—Iris A., Grade 5, *Main Street Middle School*

When my Dog Rolls Around

I love when my dog rolls around
She digs her paws into the ground
Bark, Bark, Bark! She looks at me
Then both of us are filled with glee.

—Obi B., Grade 5, *Main Street Middle School*

Dawn

The sky is lightened
A nearby stream runs faster
I awake slowly

—*Scarlett C., Grade 5, Main Street Middle School*

The Wind in the City

The wind runs through the city
    passing by cars
        trees
            and houses.

—*Kai D., Grade 5, Main Street Middle School*

Birds

Birds flying so high
Above everybody else
Those show offs with wing

—*Lowell F., Grade 5, Main Street Middle School*

Jeep

Diamond sky day
Forest drive

Wind whistling
Key glistening

The car was clobbered, clocked, and cracked by the
     nightmares — SMASH!
Then came the
Rickety gate
The great escape

The jeep grew wings and flew up high
Into the vast and pretty, diamond sky
And finally it went and saw
As far as the eye can see

The truth as bright as the pretty, diamond sky

—Isa Lyall G., Grade 5, Main Street Middle School

Known and Unknown

Things are unknown to the world
Things are known to the world
But what is the difference
Between known and unknown
Some people know
But some people don't
Small people don't know anything but Themselves
Older people say that they are wise
And know everything else
But what is the difference between
Known and unknown and knowing things

—Sarah J., Grade 5, Main Street Middle School

Blossoms

Cherry Blossom Tree
Beautiful bright pink flowers
A calm sign of spring

—Mav K., Grade 5, Main Street Middle School

Tomorrow

Not today, not yesterday, tomorrow
Not now, not when, tomorrow
Tomorrow is as blank as a page and ready to be written on.
Darkness (a different poem)
The still sky blackens
The white as milk moon rising
Soon the sun will come

—*Esther M., Grade 5, Main Street Middle School*

Mia

Mia was as skinny as a pencil unlike Jimmy.
Mia will Hiss! Hiss! Hiss! at her brother Scout until he
    leaves her alone.

—*Kinley M., Grade 5, Main Street Middle School*

Snow Day

The snow glows as bright as the sun
Putting on gloves and yanking on snow boots
Children are out to play and have fun
They race inside as the days almost done

—*Mila M., Grade 5, Main Street Middle School*

Basketball

Dribbled the ball at the speed of light.
The basketball goes dribble, dribble.
A scared face came across the ball's face.

—*Adler N., Grade 5, Main Street Middle School*

View

The wide-spreading fields
Beneath the mountain so high
The sun is hidden

—*Ned O., Grade 5, Main Street Middle School*

Dead Life

How can we know
Where to go
When all our life is lost?

Whether it ended with another
Perhaps a mother or brother
Or maybe two paths wrongly crossed?

Life feels like an eternity
When in reality
It can all go in a pop!

But as familiar weeps hang in the air
Everything is simply full of despair
Then your living death wants only to stop.

And the endless black
That goes until the crack
Awaiting you.

The dark is still a mystery
Resting 'till it greets you again
Resting 'till the dead take you.

Take you again
'Till the living dead
Take you once more.

—*Iris P., Grade 5, Main Street Middle School*

My Cat Uhtred

(Uhtred is pronounced OOO-tred)

My cat Uhtred
white as moonbeams,
with grey splotches,
drifting clouds.

His spirit is gentle as the breeze,
 though his meow can be quite loud

As warmly as the sunrise,
he purrs his sweet tune.
My cat Uhtred,
white as the moon

—Connor Q. R., Grade 5, Main Street Middle School, Montpelier

Main Street Middle School, Montpelier:
Animal Poems

The animal in me

The animal in me is a luna moth
I keep to myself like a luna moth
I don't like new environments like a luna moth
I love the night like a luna moth
I defend myself like a luna moth
I would sleep all day like a luna moth, if i could
I fly high like a luna moth
I am fragile like a luna moth
I am colorful and creative like a luna moth
The animal in me is a luna moth

—*anonymous mushrooms, Grade 6, Main Street Middle School*

Animal in me

There is a horse in me
Cool, like the breeze, warm, like the sun
You hurt me, I hurt you
I'll throw you like I kick off a shoe
my mane is soft like my heart
I am a work of art
I'm agile like the breeze as I brush past
I promise you I can run fast
I can run a thousand miles
But, I cannot shuffle files
I cannot stand still
When the trumpet sounds
With that I have to go,
But being here has been a show.

—*Asia, Grade 6, Main Street Middle School*

Animal in me: Arctic Fox

There is a Arctic fox in me
They love the cold temperature
Their friendly, playful and cheeky
Their super fast
Their adventuress
Lazy and upbeat
Cunning
Eyes like a gem in a cave
Invisible in the snow
As skittish as a cat their call as loud as an elephant
Tiny and soft
Big and rough
There is an arctic fox in me

—*Avery, Grade 6, Main Street Middle School*

There is an animal in me

There is a coyote in me
   It has sharp claws like knives
   There fast and when they run it feel the wind
There fur is like a blanket
Resourceful like me
I wish I could be a coyote
It lives in my heart
They are smart like a person
They make me feel warm inside
There quiet when they're hunting
and when there not they're loud

—*Haven Axelrod, Grade 6, Main Street Middle School*

I am a goat

There is a goat in me,
Inquisitive and smart,
With a very large heart.

Always making some kind of noise,
Climbing around with beautiful poise.

I am a goat,
Always to gloat,
With those who aren't in my boat.

Hornes,
Splotches,
Eyes like squares,
And happy to care,

For those we love.

—*Lydia Bearsch, Grade 6, Main Street Middle School*

The animal in me

I'm like a cat always wanting to chat
Shy but never telling a lie
I'm a loyal friend And Making people happy is what I Intend
 Warm and soft and can never be bossed
I'm always showing my confidence And if your mean to one
    of my friends you will take the consequence. Can't be
    Tamed and not ashamed
Some times unfriendly some people resent me
Im nice but if you are mean to me you will pay the price
Always wanting to play all day
Never letting you down never showing a frown

—Bridget, Grade 6, Main Street Middle School

Animal In Me: Giraffe

There is a giraffe in me
Giraffes are big and tall
Giraffes hardly need any sleep
Giraffes are surprisingly smart
I have long legs like a giraffe
Crunch, Crunch, Crunch
That's the sound of a giraffe
I love to eat just like a giraffe
There is a giraffe in me
And all my friends agree

—Ollie Briere, Grade 6, Main Street Middle School

Penguin in me

There's a PENGUIN in me
calm, as playful
Fast in the water toddles on land
Intelligent but self conscious
Part of a colony a big colony
Black and white like an old TV
Eye like dark pools
A chirping fills the air
Splitting though the water like a bullet
There's a penguin in me

—Kiersten, Grade 6, Main Street Middle School

African wild dog

African wild dog, oh what a sight,
With energy and mischief, day and night.
Your playful spirit, it never fades,
A bundle of joy, with a wagging tail.

Your fur so bright, like the sun in the sky,
Your eyes so bright, with a twinkle in them, why.
You chase and run, with such graceful ease,
A true marvel, of nature's breeze.

With a bark and a howl, you make your call,
Your pack, your family, stand tall.
Together you roam, wild and free,
A true delight, for you and me.

Your antics, oh so playful and fun,
A never-ending dance, under the sun.
With each leap and bound, you show your glee,
A true wild dog, a wonder to see.

—*Camrynn, Grade 6, Main Street Middle School*

The Animal in Me

There is a dragon in me
Pebbled scales, river stones
Fiery breath or frozen chill
Dragon of the sea in me, dangerous deadly tsunami
Dragon of the mud in me, ever strong and kind
Dragon of the ice in me, loyal smart protective
Dragon of the forest rain in me, as gentle as a butterfly
Dragon of the sand in me, quick wit and calculation
Dragon of the sky in me fly high soar free a lifted soul
Dragon of the dark in me sly smart trickster quick thinking
Thief

—*Ayla D., Grade 6, Main Street Middle School*

There is a mouse in me

Snakes and raccoons give me the creeps
But every once and a while I give them a little peek !
But My favorite thing of all is nibbling crumbs and
Collecting trinkets.
As i go about my life you can hear me talking,
squeak squeak squeak as i sneak sneak sneak
Im small and miniscule
And i almost never go shopping
But i manage to script and scrunch
And i alway find something for lunch

—*EJ, Grade 6, Main Street Middle School*

There is a kitten in me

I am playful like a kitten
I have softness like a mitten
With curiosity similar to a bird
And complicated like a password
Stealthy like a squirrel
And comparable to a pearl
A non-stop energy ball
And very very small
THERE IS A KITTEN IN ME!!!

—Eme!!!, Grade 6, Main Street Middle School

There is a panda in me

They are cute and furry
I am as lazy as a pond on a beautiful day
You can hear the crunch,crunch,crunch of the bamboo
Pandas play poker playfully
I am as camouflaged as a pin in a haystack
They are funny and curious
They like to sleep in the open
They are black and white
We both eat a ton

—Emmett, Grade 6, Main Street Middle School

I have a guppy in me

I am very playful and love to be with friends.

I'm small but fast and I love to feast.

My colors are unique and one of a kind.

Once you see me I'm very curious you'll find.

The first time you see me I will hide and be more scared
and shy than a house cat outside.

Every day like a guppy I'm as happy as a puppy.

I don't like new things but once I find the good inside I will
feel at ease and filled with pride.

I need much love and attention so I feel nice and warm.

I love to be happy and I will make you feel the same too.

Im am very famous, the most known fish in the school.

—*Kamryn, Grade 6, Main Street Middle School*

There is an animal in me

There is an animal in me, A soft & sweet bunny.

With loving eyes, kind nature, and silky fur as soft as clouds.

A bunny lives in my head creating my life ahead of my path.

As quiet as I am and as docile as I can be

Shy and affectionate- with a hum that sounds of wind

Like a fox dolls stalk me.

I keep my tail to myself and get ready for the day!

Like a wolf, people scare me.

I stay an introvert as no one understands me.

—*Kaz, Grade 6, Main Street Middle School*

Soup

There is a tiger in me
I am as calm as a cat
But as ferocious as a lion
I am dangerous but funny
I smell like blood
I have a calm but
Strong voice
I Am mysterious
I have a soft personality
But a fierce composure
I jump on a lump to hunt
There is a tiger in me.

—Grey Kirklink, Grade 6, Main Street Middle School

---

red wolf

There is a Red wolf in me.
As shy as an aardvark
And as protective as an elephant
And very caring for their families
The red wolf has long slender legs
The red wolf likes to hunt alone
And only likes small groups
All of these things represent me
That's why there is a Red wolf in me

—Lilyana, Grade 6, Main Street Middle School

There's a dolphin in me.

There's a dolphin in me,
It lives in the sea, agile, and joyful
There's a dolphin in me, investigating,
While others may hide.
Most bold and social,
But some can be shy,
Still agile, and curious.
Gray, black, white, two flippers, a fin,
Dolphins have smooth, rubbery skin.
There's a dolphin in me, as smart as a crow,
They're very fast, not at all slow.
There's a dolphin in me, it lives in the sea,
Agile and joyful, there's a dolphin in me.

—Revyn Lowe, Grade 6, Main Street Middle School

Baseball lion

Baseball lion roars,
Majestic on the diamond,
King of the outfield.

Golden mane shining,
Glove a fierce and steady paw,
Catching dreams with ease.

Muscles strong and swift,
Running bases like a storm,
Graceful, yet powerful.

Batter swings in fear.
As the lion eyes the ball,
Ready to strike out.

Fans roar with delight
Cheering for their mighty king
Victory assured.

Baseball lion proud
In his realm he reigns supreme
Master of the game.

—*Ethan Lynch, Grade 6, Main Street Middle School*

Animal in Me

There is a lab in me.

Labs are clumsy, and like to have fun,
They like to play outside in the sun.

Curious as a cat with a new toy,
Fun as a water slide on a summer day.

We both love sports,

Labs are great, labs are cool,
Labs, (like me) love the pool

Labs
Love
Learning

There is a lab in me

—Madeleine, Grade 6, Main Street Middle School

The squirrel in me

The squirrel in me is has brownish blonde hair
 and a mischievous smile,
The squirrel in me is silly and bold
The squirrel in me is really social,
In the summertime is really when I come out,
My true colors and fun personality,
winter is when i settle down and focus on my school and sports,
just like a squirrel,
spending the summer collecting food,
but in winter settling down and focusing on staying alive.
The squirrel in me has still has a life to uphold

—Maggie, Grade 6, Main Street Middle School

Flamingo

The animal in me is a flamingo, I'm as quiet as I can be,
with one leg in the air I stand,
The waves crash at my feet as I live at the ocean
I almost lose my balance but a foot is in the sand.
Sure I talk too much but I can't really help it
I love to be loud to be happy to be friendly,
As long as I have someone to laugh with to fit in
Still those who are naturally pretty I envy
I still love how I look my hair my smile
And my friends still like me so i'm pretty sure i'm worth while
I talk and I talk and I talk and I never get bored,
As I walk down the street people smile at me, it's like a reward
So I walk and I laugh and I talk and I play,
I'm an average person just longing to be free,
And while I smile and I walk and I talk,
I still see a flamingo in me.

—Mel, Grade 6, Main Street Middle School

The mouse in me

There is a mouse in me.
We are smart and up with the moon,
And with the night we shine with glee.

There is a mouse in me.
Dairy we both like to eat,
But we also like a touch of meat.

There is a mouse in me.
Indoors we both like to live,
But unfortunately wishes we cannot give.

There is a mouse in me.
Pests we can sometimes be,
Not afraid of each other are we.

There is a mouse in me.

—Erik Mohlman, Grade 6, Main Street Middle School

animal in me

I am a cat
Sleepy like Garfield
I always want to rest
And eat, preferably pasta please.
I like my space
Hiss
Stay out of my face
I love summer vacation, it's a lot of fun
Laying about, resting in the sun
But after one or two months it's done.
That is that
I'm just a cat

—*Jonathan Mortensen, Grade 6, Main Street Middle School*

The black bear

There is a black bear in me
It is playful as a summer breeze
It always is curious, wanting to know more
It is swift

They are protective
They like the quiet peace of the woods
They are loyal

The bear is empathetic
The bear is thoughtful
The bear is ME

—*Rocco N., Grade 6, Main Street Middle School*

panther in me

There is a Panther in me
With sharp serrated claws as strong as iron
It sneaks with silent paws
It makes me silent
with silent paws it springs from its hiding spot
With its serrated claws it kills it prey with ease
It make me strong
It has teeth as strong as steel
Its fur as strong as leather
With eyes that can see 7 times farther than humans

—*Nico, Grade 6, Main Street Middle School*

There is a dolphin in me

Swims as fast as a motor boat
Smart like a genius
Thinks real hard
Smiles real fast
Whistles real loud
It lives in me
Plays like a puppy
Curious like a monkey
Please play with me
I wish I could be a dolphin to be free

—*Aedan Nolan, Grade 6, Main Street Middle School*

Animal in me

There is a goldfish in me

All lost and curious finding
 their way but they still find a
way to have fun every day.
Spaces out and stares into
nothing, just swims around
 and does nothing.
All day even sometimes
 they might feel gray all lost
 no one around till' one day
they might hit the ground.

—*Remmi, Grade 6, Main Street Middle School*

gorilla in me

Gorillas are unpretentious so am I.
 Gorillas are fun loving, so am I.
 Gorillas are adventurous so am I.
 Gorillas are gentle so am I.
 Gorillas are lazy yawwwn so am I.
 Some swing trees.
Some dream of the sea.
 Some gorillas look at the mountain tops.
 Some gorillas watch bunnies hop.
 Gorillas have family, so do I.

—*Oliver Rivet, Grade 6, Main Street Middle School*

The Animal in Me

There is a giraffe in me.
With unique spots like a zebra's stripes.
And social, like me.
There is a giraffe in me.
We are both tenacious,
And gracious.
Giraffes walk, and talk a lot, the same as me.
There is a giraffe in me.
Educated and dedicated,
Admiring and inspiring.
There is a giraffe in me.

—*Ruthie, Grade 6, Main Street Middle School*

The sheep in me

The animal in me is a sheep skipping through
meadows of Jade. I run across fields speckled with
wildflowers of the deepest blue. I enjoy the warmth
of the golden sun dappling my cream colored fur. A
gentle breeze carries the sweet scent of spring
blossoms. The animal in me is a sheep lost in their
imagination. I dream, I dream, I dream…The animal
in me is a sheep, timid and empathetic. I get hurt
from others' wounds like I got pierced with a shard
of glass. The animal in me is a sheep.

—*Satya, Grade 6, Main Street Middle School*

Otter in me

There's an otter in me,
Creativity in the sea,
Smart as a fox
Powerful as an ox.
Their meal an oyster
My world an oyster
Tricky you say?
I know the feeling I must decree.
Otter in me,
True as can be.

—Monroe Schwartz, Grade 6, Main Street Middle School

The fox in me

There is fox in me with stealth of wind
 And clever as a chimpanzee
It barks and howls
It's strong like a buffalo
 It lives in my soul
       And makes me brave
       I wish I was sneaky like it
       It makes me want to run and play
       It makes me curious
       It makes me stronger and braver.

—Owen Smart, Grade 6, Main Street Middle School

there's a black bear in me!

A black bear that's what I am.
Very small though for my kind
I am very curious if you mind.
I can eat a lot and that's what I love I am a funny animal and
    that is all that
I love i can deal with a lot no matter what I am very fast
Drowning in speed.
I can climb very well and awesome
I have a nose, yes!
 I have a good sense of smell near the forest is where I dwell.
I am a black bear, that's what you can tell.
Though I have a lot of hair.
I am socal I come with more than a pear.
I am humble and I won't complain.
 I am fair.
I have a black bear in me.

—Makai.Smith, Grade 6, Main Street Middle School

The Animal in Me

There is a Tortoise in me.
With a shell that's hard like a rock,
And quiet like a sloth.
It moves slowly around the dry desert,
Or in a wet tropical forest.
It's inquisitive and curious like me.
They're shy like me,
And they get scared easily,
And hide deep in their shells.
Sometimes, I wish I had a shell to hide in.
There is a tortoise in me.

—Lia Tarrant, Grade 6, Main Street Middle School

The Elephant in me

The Elephant in me.
The elephant in me is bold and strong,
Where the fire is contained, and is like a song.
The river of my personality has many twists and turns,
And flows right around the elephant
Elephants are curious and shy, just like me and the big blue sky.
Elephants are big and gray, tall and fun,
The elephant in me still has a life to up hold,
And they have a personality that reminds me of 24 carat gold.
I like the elephant in me
and the elephant in me could be as kind as the sea,
But I am not, we could be friends,
Or we could not.
The elephant in me is really cool,
And together we could rule the like the sky,
Just me and my elephant
A pair that will care.

—*Lena Vitti, Grade 6, Main Street Middle School*

The Dolphin in me

There is a Māui dolphin in me
Playful and kind
Fast like the wind
Curious but reserved

There is a Māui dolphin in me
Small and friendly
agile and timid
Shy yet joyed
Loyal, brave and true
A little rascal.

There is a Māui dolphin in me

—Lula Walker, Grade 6, Main Street Middle School

THE KELLOGG-HUBBARD LIBRARY (KHL) is a 501c3 nonprofit that serves as the public library for six communities in central Vermont. KHL has operated continuously as a library since 1895, with only brief interruptions for a polio epidemic in 1917, the Spanish Flu in 1918, the great flood of 1927, the Flood of 1992, and the Covid-19 pandemic of 2020. The Senator Patrick J. Leahy Wing was added in 2001. KHL currently serves the City of Montpelier and the Towns of Berlin, Calais, East Montpelier, Middlesex and Worcester. Learn more at www.kellogghubbard.org.

www.ingramcontent.com/pod-product-compliance
Lightning Source LLC
Chambersburg PA
CBHW030233120726
47903CB00005B/1472